Helping Teachers Develop

Sara Bubb is the UK's leading induction expert and has vast expertise in the CPD field. She runs many courses for different levels of school staff, assesses trainee and advanced skills teachers and is the new teacher expert for the *Times Educational Supplement.*

Sara has been seconded from the Institute of Education to the DfES as the consultant for the Chartered London Teacher initiative. She is the co-author, with Peter Earley, of *Leading and Managing Continuing Professional Development* and *Managing Teacher Workload.*

Helping Teachers Develop

Sara Bubb

TES
THE TIMES EDUCATIONAL SUPPLEMENT

P·C·P
Paul Chapman
Publishing

First published 2005

Paul Chapman Publishing
A SAGE Publications Company
1 Oliver's Yard
55 City Road
London EC1Y 1SP

SAGE Publications Inc
2455 Teller Road
Thousand Oaks, California 91320

SAGE Publications India Pvt Ltd
B-42, Panchsheel Enclave
Post Box 4109
New Delhi 110 017

Library of Congress Control Number: 2004093825

A Catalogue record for this book is available from the British
Library

ISBN 1 4129 1898 7
ISBN 1 4129 1899 5 (pbk)

Production by Deer Park Productions, Tavistock, Devon
Typeset by TW Typesetting, Plymouth, Devon
Printed in Great Britain by Cromwell Press, Trowbridge, Wiltshire
Printed on paper from sustainable resources

Contents

List of figures and tables

Acknowledgements

I would like to thank all those who helped and contributed in some way to the writing of this book, particularly Peter Earley, Kevan Bleach, David Hall, Stella Muttock, Steve Solomons, Suzy Challenger, Brian Lynch and teachers at Kingswood Primary in Tulse Hill. Thanks also to Jude Bowen and everyone at SAGE/Paul Chapman Publishing and Susan Young and Carola York at the *Times Educational Supplement* for having faith in my ability to write this book!

Most of all, I must thank my family and friends – especially Paul, Julian, Miranda, Oliver, John and Diana – for their encouragement and tolerance.

List of abbreviations

CEDP	Career Entry and Development Profile
CPD	Continuing professional development
DfES	Department for Education and Skills
GTC	General Teaching Council
GTP	Graduate teacher programme
HLTA	Higher level teaching assistant
HMI	Her Majesty's Inspectorate
HoD	Head of department
IEP	Individual education plan (for pupils with SEN)
INSET	In-service education and training
LEA	Local education authority
NCSL	National College for School Leadership
NPQH	National professional qualification for headship
NQT	Newly qualified teacher
OfSTED	Office for Standards in Education
QTS	Qualified teacher status
SEN	Special educational needs
SENCO	Special educational needs coordinator
SLT	Senior leadership team
SMT	Senior management team
STRB	School Teachers' Review Body
TA	Teaching assistant
TES	*Times Educational Supplement*
TTA	Teacher Training Agency
TDA	Training and Development Agency for schools

1

Helping Teachers Develop – Why?

> ▶ Why we should help teachers develop
> ▶ It's good for you too
> ▶ What is an effective teacher?
> ▶ Stages that teachers go through
> ▶ Structure of the book

It is fashionable to say that teaching can be the most rewarding profession there is – and it can be. We can all give examples of the pleasure of helping a child grow in knowledge and understanding, and achieve their potential. But what about the teacher? They shouldn't be excluded from the benefits of lifelong learning because of their workload and desire to give, give, give. Growth and change are part of all our personal and professional lives, and teachers need to embrace them; not just to do a better job, but to enjoy doing it. Supporting teachers in their development – trainees, newly or recently qualified, in their first three, ten or twenty years, and whether they're superb or struggling – is vital in improving the quality of teaching and learning in our schools.

Why we should help teachers develop

 Helping teachers develop? Why should we? Don't we have enough to do teaching children?

I'm sure the fact that you've started reading this book means that you don't need to be convinced of the reasons for helping teachers develop. For the sake of the profession, for the teachers being helped – for the millions of children who will learn more as a result – it must happen. But teaching isn't easy, and getting better at it isn't just a matter of experience, of trial and error. Not that it isn't happening already but some opportunities to further teachers' development are not being fully exploited.

Not only is helping teachers develop an intrinsically good thing but the government also wants to see more coaching of teachers by teachers. Its *Five Year Strategy for*

Children and Learners (DfES, 2004a) plans to boost demand for coaching and other forms of continuing professional development by turning teacher appraisals into teaching and learning reviews. The idea is to make sure teachers receive the development that matches their needs and that career progression and financial rewards go to those who are continually building on their own expertise. It says: 'The record on tackling the development needs of teachers will be critical to school self-evaluation and assessment' (2004a). School self-evaluation and the short-notice inspections every three years mean that people need to have an accurate picture of the quality of teaching and learning in their schools – and be constantly looking for ways to improve it.

Who needs developing? I hope this book will be useful for people helping any teacher develop, whether they're a trainee, NQT, experienced or excellent teacher, because the principles are the same. Statistically, you're most likely to be working with new teachers: in 2004–5 there were 17,450 people training to teach in primary schools and 20,820 training for secondary schools (DfES, 2005a) and every year about 20,000 teachers go through their induction year.

There is more school-based training going on than ever before, and though it is mostly well intended, not all of it is good. Phil Revell, teacher and journalist, found that a quarter of his sample of trainees found no welcome mat in their placement schools: there was no tour of the school, no information pack, no induction process to introduce them to the school and its procedures (2005b: 27). However, something's going well because everyone – inspectors and heads – agrees that new teachers are very effective.

 The department seems to have little or no camaraderie and they are phenomenally unwelcoming to student teachers. I get bullied by one class teacher and criticized for the most trivial things by the others. They never have a good word to say about anything I do.

Even where schools have a statutory duty to provide support, monitoring and assessment for teachers in their induction year the picture is patchy. Newly qualified teachers should have:

- A 10 per cent lighter teaching timetable than other teachers in the school;

- A job description that doesn't make unreasonable demands;

- Meetings with the school 'induction tutor' including half-termly reviews of progress;

- An individualized programme of support, monitoring and assessment;

- Objectives, informed by strengths and areas for development identified in the career entry and development profile, to help them meet the induction standards;

- At least one observation of their teaching each half term with oral and written feedback;

- An assessment meeting and report at the end of each term;

■ Procedures to air grievances at school and local education authority level (Bubb et al., 2005: 252).

But in 2002, research found that a quarter of new teachers weren't getting their whole entitlement (Totterdell et al., 2002) and I'm not sure it's any better now; in fact it may be worse. Some people have fantastic experiences and couldn't want for better support but here are four new teachers' rather shocking views of their induction tutors:

Teacher A:	'My induction tutor is a bitch who has reduced me to a nervous wreck. It's got to the point where I can't teach in front of her because I'm convinced I'll fail.'
Teacher B:	'My tutor is constantly on my back and tells me off when I don't do exactly what she says.'
Teacher C:	'Mine is never there. He has a mug with "I'm so effing cool" on it and a picture of a guy in a hammock smoking a spliff. He calls the kids half-wits.'
Teacher D:	'I am not getting on well with my induction tutor's forthright manner. She treats me as if I am a total newcomer (I have been working in informal education for seven years). She does not seem to believe in any basic mentoring feedback methods and really only gives positives or achievements in written feedback after verbal negatives. She has made me cry twice and often does not accept any of my version or explanations for events. I feel that she is watching my every move for something she can pick up on, rather than things she can put as achievements.'

Even potentially strong NQTs in supportive schools with trained induction tutors don't find things easy. Rosie Warden, who was featured on Teachers' TV, is a case in point. She really enjoyed her PGCE course and finished on a high with good experiences on teaching practice and lots of positive feedback. She thought she'd spend her first year consolidating her learning and going from strength to strength. She'd been warned that the children were 'challenging', but on visits to the school she'd always seen experienced teachers, so didn't fully appreciate what she would be up against: 'The reality is that behaviour management has been tough for me'.

But what about staff who don't take responsibility for their development? We've all met people who see training as time off, who think they've nothing more to learn, who are unreflective, and who don't consider how their professional development might affect pupils. 'New Professionalism' is not new but an expectation right from the word go. One of the standards for Qualified Teacher Status is that:

Teachers are able to improve their own teaching, by evaluating it, learning from the effective practice of others and from evidence. They are motivated and able to take increasing responsibility for their own professional development. (TTA, 2003: 12)

People need to have wider professional effectiveness to cross the threshold, taking 'responsibility for their professional development and use the outcomes to improve their teaching and pupils' learning, and make an active contribution to the policies and aspirations of the school' (DfES, 2004c: 3).

Part of the reason why some people don't take their own development seriously is that in many schools it's not thought through well enough. If 'personalization' is what we're expected to do for pupils how can CPD be personalized for staff? How does one marry up tensions between what an individual wants to develop with school improvement and national initiatives? England's GTC says there should be an entitlement to CPD throughout a teacher's career and one that is not linked solely to school targets. Its *Teachers' Professional Learning Framework* says teachers need the opportunity to:

- Have structured time to engage in sustained reflection and structured learning;

- Create learning opportunities from everyday practice;

- Develop their ability to identify their own learning and development needs and those of others;

- Develop an individual learning plan;

- Have school-based learning recognized for accreditation;

- Develop self-evaluation, observation and peer review skills;

- Develop mentoring and coaching skills;

- Plan their longer-term career aspirations (2003: 6).

It's good for you too

Many people who work in a mentoring role enjoy it, saying it's the best part of their many roles and they get a lot from it, as this induction tutor says:

> In the vast majority of cases, they're young people who are enthusiastic, enjoy their work, and you know I find it very refreshing and I learn from watching them. I think this is the thing that's perhaps surprising, an experienced teacher can go and watch an NQT and still pick up some tricks. (cited in Bubb et al., 2002: 68)

Until now, however, helping teachers develop has been a rather low-status role with few financial rewards. Things should change now that professional development is back on the agenda. The DfES, GTC and Training and Development Agency for schools (TDA) have placed an emphasis on well-planned and high-quality continuing professional development (CPD) for teachers as a way of raising standards of teaching and learning, and retaining high-quality staff. There's more of a focus on CPD for all staff – not just teachers but support and admin staff too – and a greater link with performance management through 'teaching and learning reviews'.

There are also career progression and rewards because progress on the upper pay scale will depend not only on teachers showing that they have developed themselves but also that they are coaching and mentoring less experienced teachers. Those hoping to gain the new excellent teacher status will also have to demonstrate that they have provided regular coaching and mentoring to colleagues. People achieving the grade of excellent teacher will be expected to be involved in:

- The induction of newly qualified teachers;

- Professional mentoring of other teachers;

- Sharing good practice through demonstration lessons;

- Helping teachers to develop their expertise in planning, preparation and assessment;

- Helping other teachers to evaluate the impact of their teaching on pupils;

- Undertaking classroom observations to assist and support the performance management process; and

- Helping teachers improve their teaching practice including those on capability procedures.

Collaboration within and between schools is the name of the game. CPD will increasingly be school based, with people coaching and mentoring others. Sounds interesting, but is it going to work? It could just be too cosy and result in staleness unless there's agreement on what an effective teacher is.

What is an effective teacher?

Before one starts helping teachers develop it is important to have a clear understanding of what an effective teacher is. This seems simple but in fact it's the subject of much debate. Teachers who have been in the profession a long time will be aware of the fashion element to this but you need to have some knowledge of the current OfSTED criteria for teaching and the standards for higher-level teaching assistants, qualified teacher status, induction, threshold, subject leaders, SENCOs, headteachers and excellent teacher and advanced skills teacher status.

As a taster, let us look at the induction standards which, like those for QTS, are organized under the following headings:

1. Professional values and practice;

2. Knowledge and understanding;

3. Teaching:
    (a) Planning, expectations and targets
    (b) Monitoring and assessment
    (c) Teaching strategies and behaviour.

As well as meeting the QTS standards consistently, NQTs must meet these six standards. They must:

1. Seek and use opportunities to work collaboratively with colleagues to raise standards by sharing effective practice in the school;

2. Show a commitment to their professional development by identifying areas in which they need to improve their professional knowledge, understanding and practice in order to teach more effectively in their current post, and with support, taking steps to address these needs;

3. Plan effectively to meet the needs of pupils with special educational needs, with or without statements and, in consultation with the SENCO, contribute to the preparation, implementation, monitoring and review of Individual Education Plans or the equivalent;

4. Liaise effectively with parents or carers on pupils' progress and achievements;

5. Work effectively as part of a team and, as appropriate to the post in which they are completing induction, liaise with, deploy, and guide the work of other adults who support pupils' learning;

6. Secure a standard of behaviour that enables pupils to learn, and act to pre-empt and deal with inappropriate behaviour in the context of the behaviour policy of the school (TTA, 2003a).

Do these make you – like me – shrivel with inadequacy because I'm not sure I would meet them, after more than 20 years in the job! In fact ex-HMI Colin Richards (2000) wrote, not entirely flippantly:

> The standards represent an impossible set of demands which properly
> exemplified would need the omnicompetence of Leonardo da Vinci, the
> diplomatic expertise of Kofi Annan, the histrionic skills of Julie Walters, the
> grim determination of Alex Ferguson, and the saintliness of Mother Teresa,
> coupled with the omniscience of God.

We all know what we should be – the perfect parent, partner, lover, teacher – but no one can be perfect all the time so we need to think about what is a good enough teacher. I think that liking children is of prime importance and yet it does not feature in any standards, possibly because it is hard to measure and assumed to be a given. Yet, I'm sure we can all think of some teachers who do not enjoy and feel irritated by being with certain age groups. Professionalism implies more than meeting a series of discrete standards. Teaching demands creativity, commitment, energy and enthusiasm and the intellectual and managerial skills. Do you think these are shown in this lesson?

> In a science lesson, the teacher stimulated the pupils' interest through an imaginative and provocative piece of planning. Pupils entered the classroom to find a 'body' on the floor with smears of powder. The task was to use their existing scientific knowledge to solve the 'crime'. The teacher's lively manner and humorous approach both engaged pupils and gave them confidence to participate. Very clear and brisk instructions challenged pupils and left them in no doubt what they had to do, setting out high expectations of their behaviour and cooperative working skills. They set to the task with great enthusiasm, and no little controlled excitement, testing a range of powders accessible to different 'suspects'. Tests included those for solubility, acidity and alkalinity; and reaction with water and reaction with a mild acid. From their knowledge of the properties of the different powders pupils found the answer to their first piece of forensic science, that Mr Cook the baker had done the dastardly deed. Not only did pupils attain the expected standard in organizing their own investigation, recording their findings and working together but also they achieved well. (OfSTED, 2005)

The standards are not things that once achieved are mastered for all time – if they can ever truly be achieved. They should be seen on a continuum because each has a vast potential within which teachers can develop and challenge themselves, and each change of context may result in deceleration or acceleration along the continuum. It would be useful for people involved with helping teachers develop to discuss what can be realistically expected at each stage of a career in their context. It will vary but the key concern is that attention moves from teaching on to learning and on to more effective learning.

Stages that teachers go through

In addition to thinking about what a good teacher is in your particular school setting, you should also consider what stage the teachers you are working with are at. There are certain stages that new teachers go through. Recognizing them will help you realize that teachers need different levels and types of support at different times. Like any skill or craft, learning to teach is a developmental process characterized by devastating disasters and spectacular successes. Teaching is a job that can never be done perfectly – one can always improve. This is what makes it such a great job – but also such a potentially depressing one.

How people feel about teaching will probably change daily at first. One day will be great and leave them feeling positive and idealistic, but the next will be diabolical. As time goes on good days outnumber the bad ones, and eventually people realize that they are actually enjoying the job. Appreciating this will help you realize that people will need different levels and types of support at different times during their career.

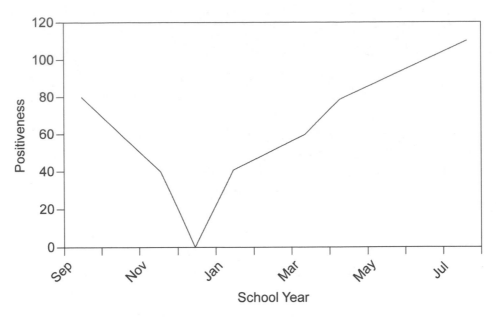

Figure 1.1 *NQTs' feelings during the year*

Figure 1.1 has a trajectory of teachers' typical feelings during their first year. They start on a high in September but then reality strikes and they live from day to day, needing quick fixes and tips for survival. It's hard to solve problems because there are so many of them. Behaviour management is of particular concern but they're too stressed and busy to reflect. Colds and sore throats seem permanent. Getting through all the Christmas activities is exhausting. In January, pupils return calmer and ready to work. Teachers can identify difficulties and think of solutions because there is some space in their life. Then they feel that they're mastering teaching, begin to enjoy it but don't want to tackle anything different or take on any radical new initiatives. Eventually, people will be ready for further challenges, want to try out different styles of teaching, new age groups, take more responsibilities.

Structure of the book

I wrote this book to help people support individual teachers' development. It contains findings from the most recent research and real examples of current good practice, as well as practical formats. In the appendix there are blank copies of some of the sheets shown in the book. I have used postings from the *TES* website's virtual staffroom (indicated by a mouse symbol) to illustrate real situations: how teachers feel about their support, the issues they face and what has helped them.

The first thing to explore is how to go about developing teachers so Chapter 2 looks at how adults learn and how the professional development cycle works, before considering how to analyse needs, set objectives and draw up action plans.

Chapter 3 considers what good professional development looks like and explores a range of ways teachers can develop through activities such as coaching and mentoring, learning conversations, self study, observing other teachers, courses and being observed.

Observation is a powerful tool for assessing and monitoring a teacher's progress. Used well, it can also be a way to support teachers, because observation gives such a detailed picture and enables very specific help to be given. Chapter 4 considers what is good practice in setting up an observation, what proformas to use and what to do during the observation and after the lesson, with the discussion. Putting pen to paper can be hard so I have included an analysis of different people's written feedback on a range of lessons, from the excellent to the unsatisfactory.

However, observation is not the only way to monitor and help. Chapter 5 considers how to help teachers with planning, deploying support staff, writing individual education plans and reports. It includes some examples of feedback on these crucial areas because this is where an experienced and supportive mentor can really make a difference.

We should always remember that because teachers are people too, they cannot live on good will alone, and they cannot devote themselves forever to just one job. Nor is this a bad thing: true professional development in the longer term demands personal goals, progression and variety, and every teacher should be encouraged to think about the next step as carefully as possible. This can be one of the hardest acts of all, both for the professional concerned and those whose job it is to advise them. I have included material on this in Chapter 6 because I am convinced that a constructively career-minded approach is, in the end, a great benefit to teachers, their schools, the profession as a whole, and the children we are all seeking to help.

I hope that whenever a teacher feels 'there's so much more I want to give', there will be someone who wants to help them do just that. And if this book can assist that process I'll be very happy!

2

How to Develop People

 My mentor was brilliant! Basically she understood and remembered what it was like to train. She would be in the class for the first few lessons – but always doing some work so I didn't feel she was just watching me – then she would not be around as often, which gave me lots of confidence. I always knew where she was if I needed her. She spent a lot of time early on showing me all of the resources in the classroom and told me where other things were if I might need them. We talked about the topics I would be doing and she offered some suggestions as to what might work or might not. At the end of every day we would discuss how it went and if I needed anything for the next day. Every Friday after school we would have a planning/brainstorm meeting where we would discuss what I would be doing the next week. She never made me feel I was being a nuisance if I asked her anything.

Developing teachers is not easy to do. Training is comparatively easy but for deep and lasting learning to take place, it is normally more effective not to be explicitly directive but to listen and 'coach' people. You need to ask the questions that help them reflect upon why things might have happened and how they can approach things most effectively to find their own solutions. This takes a great deal of 'emotional' intelligence – understanding how other people are feeling and reading between the lines – because you don't need to be an expert all the time but you do need to help people take ownership of their development and problems. So, it's useful to have a thorough view of the professional development cycle and think about how adults learn before getting into the nitty gritty of identifying needs.

The professional development cycle

The professional development cycle consists of six stages: identifying and analysing needs, designing and implementing some professional development, monitoring it and evaluating its impact. The stages are shown in Figure 2.1. The first two stages are the

11

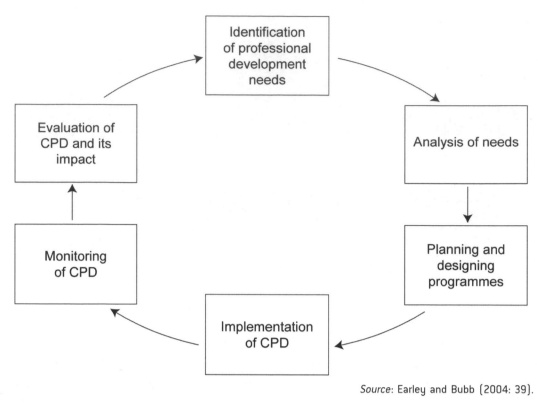

Source: Earley and Bubb (2004: 39).

Figure 2.1 *The professional development cycle*

identification of needs and their analysis, taking into account what teachers already know and can do. Identifying and analysing needs can be time consuming but the effort is worthwhile. The next challenge is to find the best way to meet needs: the range of professional development activities is huge, as we shall see in the next chapter. The final stages in the staff development cycle – monitoring and evaluating the impact of professional development and training – are neglected areas. Monitoring activities are concerned with ensuring that things are going according to plan and meeting needs, and taking appropriate action if they are not. Gauging the impact of CPD or evaluating its effectiveness on teacher behaviour or pupils' learning – the sixth and last stage in the staff development cycle – is much more difficult.

An American, Tom Guskey (2002), has done some important work in this field. He identifies five levels of evaluation of CPD with improved pupil outcomes being the desired end result:

1. Participants' reactions;

2. Participants' learning;

3. Organization support and change – the key role that the school can play in supporting or sabotaging any CPD efforts;

4. Participants' use of new knowledge and skills;

5. Pupil learning outcomes.

This can be adapted to these levels of impact, as illustrated in Box 2.1:

- *Level One*: Immediate reaction;

- *Level Two*: Learning, networks, confidence;

- *Level Three*: Putting things into practice;

- *Levels Four and Five*: Impact on pupils and then other teachers, or teachers and then pupils.

Box 2.1   The levels of impact of Jill's one-day induction tutor training course

Level One: Immediate reaction
Despite the day being well organized and in pleasant surroundings, Jill did not enjoy it because she had to sit next to and work with her ex-husband's second wife – the woman her husband left her for!

Level Two: Learning, networks, confidence
However, she gained much new knowledge and increased her skills. She felt more confident in the role of induction tutor. The extensive handouts reminded her of her learning and provided easy-to-use systems.

Level Three: Putting things into practice
Jill used her newly gained knowledge, skills and confidence in working with the two NQTs.

Level Four: Impact on teachers
The NQTs said that the school's induction was initially poor but improved after Jill attended the course. They really noticed a difference because of all the new systems and found their induction very effective. They felt well supported, and monitored and assessed fairly so that they were able to make good progress in their first year.

Level Five: Impact on pupils
This had an impact on the NQTs' pupils who learned more and behaved better as a result of improved teaching by their inexperienced teachers.

The end result of helping teachers develop should be that they are happier and more effective so that their pupils learn better. We know a lot about what helps and hinders children's learning – but how do adults learn?

How adults learn

Thinking about how adults learn is crucial for anyone involved in helping teachers develop. The way that we understand learning will affect the provision of activities we make for people to learn, and the accuracy of our understanding will affect the effectiveness of the learning that takes place. Teachers have a wide variety of previous experiences, knowledge, skills, interests and competences. The American writer Knowles, who was the first to use the term 'andragogy' as opposed to pedagogy, believes that adults need to know why they need to learn something, to learn experientially, approach learning as problem solving, and learn best when the topic is of immediate value. He also noted the following characteristics of adult learners:

- They are largely self-directed and require a climate of trust, openness, respect and collaboration to learn effectively;

- The previous experience of the learner has to be implicit in the learning process (it's too significant to ignore);

- The adult learner needs to accept the need to learn;

- They are biased towards problem solving as a learning activity;

- Practical relevance is a significant factor in gaining commitment;

- They only internalize learning if motivated by intrinsic factors (in Earley and Weindling, 2004: 175).

Any school will have a variety of people working within it, with a range of experience and needs who vary in the effectiveness of their teaching. Kathryn Riley (2003) distinguishes two extremes of teachers, whom she calls the 'Glow worms' and 'Skylarks':

- 'Glow worms' are cautious and lack spontaneity, caught up in a 'painting by numbers approach to teaching'. Nevertheless, the 'glow' of teaching is still there, however dimly lit and however intermittent – it just needs to be fanned and nurtured.

- 'Skylarks' talk about the need to put the 'sparkle' back into teaching. They are keen on sharing good practice with colleagues in other schools, having sabbaticals and secondments; participating in international and professional exchange programmes.

I'm sure glow-worms and skylarks irritate each other immensely yet it's useful to consider where the people you're helping develop sit on the spectrum between these extremes – and the implications of how to approach their learning. Frank Coffield (2005) believes that 'it's no longer sufficient for leadership teams to know how students learn; they need to know how to promote their own learning and that of colleagues. There must be dedicated time and training for teachers to learn'.

Experiential learning is important for adults: the cycle of 'do, review, learn and apply' (Dennison and Kirk, 1990). So, someone who wants to get better at taking assembly, for instance, might usefully go through the cycle in this way:

Do	Observe someone that I admire take assembly
Review	Think about it and discuss it with them afterwards
Learn	Learn some key techniques for taking assembly
Apply	Try them out when I take assembly
Do	Get someone to observe me taking assembly and give me feedback.

Learning styles

Considering learning styles in education is very fashionable. Howard Gardner's notion of multiple intelligences and our awareness of children who are predominantly visual, auditory or kinaesthetic learners is useful in our teaching reminding us of the need to present information using all three styles. Professor Coffield (2005), however, offers a warning:

> Some of the learning styles instruments – many of them well-known commercial products – make extravagant claims of success which are not upheld when subjected to scrutiny. Furthermore, people who use these instruments may come to think in stereotypes. The real danger is that if learners think they are a 'low auditory, kinaesthetic learner', they might see little point in reading a book or listening to anyone for more than a few minutes.

Bearing this in mind, do you think different adults learn in different ways and have preferred learning styles? Well, many people have investigated this area and it will be useful for anyone helping teachers develop to know some key ideas.

Probably the best known analysis of adult learning styles is that of Honey and Mumford (2000). They identify four types of learners who prefer to learn in different ways:

– *The Theorist*: likes to learn using abstract conceptualization and reflective observation (lecture, papers, analogies) and ask such questions as: 'How does this relate to that?'
   Training approach: case studies, theory readings, thinking alone.

– *The Pragmatist*: likes to learn using abstract conceptualization and active experimentation (laboratories, fieldwork, observations). Pragmatists ask: 'How can I apply this in practice?'
   Training approach: peer feedback and activities that apply skills.

– *The Activist*: likes to learn using concrete experience and active experimentation (simulations, case study, homework). Activists tell themselves: 'I'm game for anything'.
   Training approach: practising the skill, problem solving, small group discussions, peer feedback.

– *The Reflector*: likes to learn using reflective observation and concrete experience (logs, journals, brainstorming). Reflectors like time to think about the subject.
   Training approach: lectures with plenty of reflection time.

Honey and Mumford have a questionnaire designed to help people pinpoint their learning preferences so that they are in a better position to select learning experiences that suit them. Few people fall neatly into one category, but have a leaning towards one or two. However, it's useful for teachers to know where their preferences lie and for people organizing professional development to take this into account.

When Clare, an induction tutor, filled in the questionnaire she was identified very strongly as an Activist with only minimal aspects of Reflector, Pragmatist and Theorist. The newly qualified teacher she was supporting was however almost opposite to her – strongly a Reflector and Theorist with low scores as an Activist. This was a 'Road to Damascus' learning moment for Clare because she realized that the advice she'd been giving to her NQT hadn't been working because she hadn't considered what a different sort of learner he was.

The style of courses is something to take into consideration. Geoff Brookes (2004), a deputy says,

> Constant change brings with it a necessity to keep up to date, to be re-educated. But when I do go on a course these days, I am offered party games. Perhaps I have been unlucky, but I do not need to introduce myself to five people I don't already know. I do not need role-play. I do not need to share my life story with a stranger. These things are purposeless and irritating.

The learning styles, habits and forms of teachers are significant because they relate so closely to their core activity at work: helping others to learn. If individual teachers understand how they learn and can appreciate that others have different learning styles then they will be more able to support the learning of both young people and colleagues.

It's often said that no two people are exactly alike, but according to one psychological theory, based on the Myers Briggs Inventory, they can share one of 16 personality types, which are formed by different combinations of personality traits: spontaneous/planner; ideas/facts; heads/hearts; and introvert/extrovert:

1. Big Thinker (Spontaneous + Ideas + Heads + Extrovert)

2. Counsellor (Planner + Ideas + Hearts + Introvert)

3. Go-getter (Spontaneous + Facts + Heads + Extrovert)

4. Idealist (Spontaneous + Ideas + Hearts + Introvert)

5. Innovator (Spontaneous + Ideas + Hearts + Extrovert)

6. Leader (Planner + Ideas + Heads + Extrovert)

7. Mastermind (Planner + Ideas + Heads + Introvert)

8. Mentor (Planner + Ideas + Hearts + Extrovert)

9. Nurturer (Planner + Facts + Hearts + Introvert)

10. Peacemaker (Spontaneous + Facts + Hearts + Introvert)

11. Performer (Spontaneous + Facts + Hearts + Extrovert)

12. Provider (Planner + Facts + Hearts + Extrovert)

13. Realist (Planner + Facts + Heads + Introvert)

14.   Resolver (Spontaneous + Facts + Heads + Introvert)

15.   Strategist (Spontaneous + Ideas + Heads + Introvert)

16.   Supervisor (Planner + Facts + Heads + Extrovert)

(see www.bbc.co.uk/science/humanbody/mind/surveys/whatamilike)

It's rather fun to complete the quiz on the BBC website (I was delighted that I came out as a leader!), and realizing that people whom I train have different personalities has given me some useful insight into what buttons to press.

People learn in different ways and have preferred learning styles but learning takes place in a variety of ways and in different settings. It can be formal or informal, within the workplace or off-site. One can also think of learning in vertical (knowing more, new learning and experiences) and horizontal dimensions (the same knowledge applied in different contexts, deeper understanding). So, teachers don't always have to learn new things to be developing professionally, but at some level they will be changing their practice. This brings me to another idea that I've found useful: the change equation.

Change equation

Martin and Holt (2002) believe that five components must be present for change to take place: vision, skills, incentives, resources and action plans. Although intended for looking at organizations, their 'change equation' is a useful model, because for teachers to develop some things will have to change. The omission of any one component can lead to problems (see Table 2.1). For instance, Amy's problem is poor behaviour in tutor group time: chatting, mucking about. We can apply the change equation to her problem:

Vision – knowing how she wants her tutor group to behave;

Skills – she has behaviour management skills that she uses successfully when teaching her subject;

Incentives – people have complained about the noise the form makes;

Resources – advice from colleagues; observation of other teachers' form times; reading articles; time to think through what she's going to do;

Action plan – drawing up a plan of what she's going to do and when.

If vision is missing, she won't develop because she doesn't know what her end goal is or what her boundaries for behaviour are in this informal time. This is very common – the 'how much should I put up with?' syndrome;

If she doesn't have the skills to improve behaviour, such as use of voice, strategies, rewards and sanctions, she'll get anxious and feel inadequate;

If there are no incentives, such as people complaining or an inspection looming, she may develop but not as quickly;

Table 2.1 *The change equation*

Vision	Skills	Incentives	Resources	Action plans	= Change
******	Skills	Incentives	Resources	Action plans	= Confusion
Vision	******	Incentives	Resources	Action plans	= Anxiety
Vision	Skills	******	Resources	Action plans	= Gradual change
Vision	Skills	Incentives	******	Action plans	= Frustration
Vision	Skills	Incentives	Resources	******	= False starts

Source: Martin and Holt (2002: 37).

If there are no *resources*, such as advice from colleagues; observation of other teachers' form times; relevant articles; or time to think through what she's going to do, she'll get frustrated;

If there is no *action plan*, written or mental, she may not get round to improving behaviour or be inconsistent. There will be lots of false starts.

Analyse needs, set objectives and draw up an action plan

Identifying learning needs is important because it really isn't that easy. The DfES now has an on-line professional development and career planning portfolio (see www.teachernet.gov.uk/development) that encourages individual reflection on CPD and career pathways. Identifying needs can be done superficially, with people saying what they want rather than what they need – or why. Most people benefit from a real analysis in order to get the help they need – but it really isn't that easy. Ralph Tabberer (2005), chief executive of the Teacher Training Agency, says: 'there is insufficient time invested in analysing the knowledge and skills that individuals could use to strengthen their teaching'. For instance, does someone with control problems need a behaviour management course? Maybe, but perhaps the root cause has to do with planning, relationships, attitude, pace or resources – all manner of things.

Questions like these, based on the Career Entry and Development Profile, help people think more deeply:

- What are your main strengths and achievements? What brought them about?

- How well are your pupils achieving? Could anything be better?

- What aspects of teaching and learning do you want to get better at? Why?

- Do you have any new roles that you need training for?

- How do you see your career panning out? What's the next step to get you there? (TTA, 2003b)

18

It is very hard to decide what to work on when things are not going right, because each problem has a huge knock on effect – and some staff have suffered from not having areas for development accurately diagnosed. Particularly when someone has a problem, it needs to be reflected upon and analysed in order to draw up the most useful objectives and plan of action. These steps are useful in analysing development needs:

1. Brainstorm the problem's features;

2. List some positive features, relating to the problem area;

3. Reflection – think about why things go well and tease out the reasons for the problem;

4. Set objectives;

5. Draw up an action plan.

Brainstorm the problem's features

It's good to look at exactly what the problem is and its consequences. For instance, newly qualified teacher Miranda's control problems included the following:

- her voice is thin and becomes screechy when raised;

- sometimes she comes down hard on the pupils and at other times she lets them get away with things;

- she takes a long time to get attention;

- she runs out of time so plenaries are missed, the class is late to assembly and so on;

- pupils call out;

- pupils are too noisy;

- a small group of pupils is behaving badly; and

- even the usually well-behaved pupils are being naughty.

When you've made the list, look at it. Does it seem a fair picture? It's easy to be too hard or too generous.

List some positive features

For instance, Miranda:

- really likes and cares for the pupils;

- speaks to them with respect;

- plans interesting work for them;

- is very effective when working with individuals or small groups;

- has better control in the early part of the day; and works hard.

Reflection time

Think about why things go well – reflection on successes is very powerful. For instance, Miranda realized that things were better in the mornings because she was fresher and had a teaching assistant with her. The process of analysing strengths is very helpful and this positive thinking can now be used to reflect on problems. It's important to diagnose the reasons for the problem – the root cause. For instance, rather than saying that 'noisy pupils cause Miranda problems', be more diagnostic: 'noise causes Miranda to overstretch her voice, which compromises her authority'. Test out your hypotheses with the teacher and anyone else who can comment.

Set objectives

 Is 'keep your room tidy' a valid professional development target for a teacher?

Once needs have been analysed it's useful to encapsulate what one wants to develop into some sort of objective or target. This will provide a framework for teachers doing a complex job at a very fast pace. Setting an objective encourages people to prioritize, be realistic, make best use of time and other resources, and feel a sense of achievement when small steps are made. The very act of writing an objective down forces people to consider whether they are the real priorities and gives them something to focus on. Keeping one's room tidy would rarely be a priority and isn't about professional development.

A frequent problem with objectives is that they are not made specific enough – 'I want to be a better teacher' – which can lead to failure. Individuals' objectives can be set within teaching and learning reviews and link in with other developments in the school such as those in the school improvement plan. For instance, in a school where a priority was 'Improve the quality of teaching in AT1 mathematics at Key Stage 2 through a comprehensive staff training programme' an individual teacher's objective was: 'Participate in training in the teaching of AT1 mathematics through school-based courses, self study and observation of other teachers'. Will participation mean that learning takes place and has an impact in the classroom? Not necessarily!

How many times have we been told that objectives should be SMART: Specific, Measurable, Achievable, Relevant and Time-bound? This is of course also true of learning objectives in lesson plans or targets on Individual Education Plans (IEPs). Unfortunately it is easier said than done. Consider an objective such as 'Improve control'. This may be too large, and could take a long time to achieve. It is better to be more specific about what needs most urgent attention. For Miranda this was 'To improve control, particularly after playtimes, in independent literacy activities, at tidying-up time, and home time within a half-term'. Is that specific, measurable, achievable, relevant and time-bound? I think so. Think of actions to remedy situations – they can be surprisingly easy. It's often the small things that make a difference.

Draw up an action plan

Once you've helped teachers choose an area to develop they need to decide how they're going to do so and draw up an action plan with dates. What budget or time allocation is there? You may think there's none, but ask around. All schools have to meet their teachers' development needs and there should be money, time and resources available, but all the funding for CPD is in schools' general budgets rather than being ringfenced. Giving schools autonomy is fine but without a strong steer some school leaders may choose not to spend money on CPD or will not spend it wisely, like the one that blew its annual allocation on an expensive weekend for the senior management team. Whatever there is, it's unlikely to be a fortune so it must be spent well for maximum impact. Think about how the teacher learns best. Choose something that's going to work for them within the timescale, whether it's reading a book, watching Teachers' TV, going on a course or observing someone's lesson.

Miranda completed a very detailed action plan (see Table 2.2). Such detail is not always necessary, though it illustrates how breaking a problem into manageable chunks helps. For her, these were:

1. to get attention more quickly;

2. to shout rarely;

3. to plan for behaviour management;

4. to set up procedures for
    (a) sorting out disputes after playtimes
    (b) tidying
    (c) home time
    (d) independent literacy activities.

Her professional development didn't cost much: one course on voice management and lots of observation and discussion. The impact, however, was great because the CPD was so finely tuned to solving Miranda's problems with managing behaviour.

Identifying and analysing needs can be time consuming but, like any in-depth look at pupils' learning needs, the effort is worthwhile. The next challenge is to find the best way to meet the identified needs, which is the subject of the next chapter, 'Professional development activities'.

Table 2.2 *An action plan to meet an objective**

Name: Miranda   *Date*: 1 November   *Date objective to be met*: 16 December

Objective: To improve control, particularly after playtimes, in independent literacy activities, at tidying-up time, and home time

Success criteria	Actions	When	Progress
Gets attention more quickly	Brainstorm attention-getting devices with other teachers. Use triangle, etc. to get attention	4.11	7.11 Triangle made children more noisy – try cymbal
Rarely shouts	Voice management course. Project the voice. Don't talk over children.	19.11	23.11 Using more range in voice – working!
Plans for behaviour management	Glean ideas from other teachers through discussion and observation. Watch videos on behaviour management strategies. Write notes for behaviour management on plans.	4.11	12.11 Improvement through lots of tips, staying calm and being more positive. Not perfect and exhausting but better.
Successful procedures for sorting out disputes after playtimes	Glean ideas from other teachers. Ask playground supervisors to note serious incidents. Children to post messages in incident box.	11.11	18.11 Incident box really working for those who can write and I can now tell when there's a serious problem.
Successful procedures for tidying	Discuss and observe what other teachers do. Start tidying earlier and time it with reward for beating record. Sanctions for the lazy.	18.11	25.11 Sandtimer for tidying working well though still a few children not helping. Might try minutes off playtime.
Successful procedures for home time	Observe and discuss ideas with other teachers. Monitors to organize things to take home. Start hometime procedures earlier and time them (with rewards?)	25.11	2.12 Changed routine so tidy earlier. Some Y6 children helping give out things to take home.
Children succeed in independent literacy activities	Ideas from literacy co-ordinator. Change seating for groups. Differentiate work. Discuss with additional adults.	2.12	9.12 All class doing same independent activity working better. Mrs H helping.

*See Photocopiable 1 for a blank version.
Source: Earley and Bubb (2004: 58).

3

Professional Development Activities

> ► What does good professional development look like?
> ► Coaching and mentoring
> ► Learning conversations
> ► Self study and Teachers' TV
> ► Observing other teachers

There is a huge range of professional development opportunities – more than ever before – and one of the challenges for people who help develop teachers is to keep up to date with what's available. The DfES has developed an electronic portfolio for teachers called *Keeping Track* (see www.teachernet.gov.uk), which provides teachers with the opportunity to build and maintain an electronic professional portfolio (an e-portfolio) by:

- showing teachers how to keep track of their own professional development;

- enabling teachers to record milestones and achievements as a basis for reflecting on progress and further development needs;

- making it easier for teachers to maintain and update records, including a CV.

It contains some suggestions for CPD opportunities especially those linked to career stages or roles, such as the National College for School Leadership's courses *Leading from the Middle* or NPQH, the national professional qualification for headship. This chapter considers what effective CPD looks like before looking at a few of the many opportunities that teachers have to help them develop.

What does good professional development look like?

The TTA says that evidence is clear about the main characteristics of CPD that appear effective in improving teachers' performance and in raising standards of pupil achievement:

- there should be a clear and agreed vision of what effective teaching looks like;

- it should be based on the best available evidence of teaching and learning;

- it should take account of participants' previous knowledge and experience;

- it should enable teachers to develop further experience in subject content, teaching strategies, uses of technology and other essential elements required for teaching to high standards;

- it should be driven by a coherent long-term plan, so that it is sustained;

- it promotes continuous inquiry and problem solving embedded in the daily life of schools;

- there should be support in the form of coaching and mentoring from experienced colleagues;

- there should be an evaluation of impact on teaching and learning, which guides subsequent professional development efforts (TTA, 2005).

Research suggests that if any single element of this prescription is absent, the impact of CPD is significantly reduced. 'In-house' professional development – networking among teachers, mentoring and coaching within the same school or group of schools – is highly effective, particularly when it is well managed and purposefully organized within a climate of openness and mutual support. People operate best, and perform to a higher level, in supportive, humane work environments with a no-blame culture, and where people admit that 'we all make mistakes'. The GTC (2003: 3) believes that: 'Teachers who collaborate, learn together, share ideas and model best practice are more likely to remain in teaching. They feel valued and supported in their development and in their work.'

Professional learning has to be given high status. What messages are sent to teachers when a training session is held after school in a grubby classroom? Abraham Moss High School in Manchester has a purpose-built Staff Development Suite consisting of a library, meeting areas and workstations, as well as flexible areas for small and large group training. It is equipped with an interactive whiteboard, printers, photocopier and scanner, together with laptops for general use. There are also audiovisual facilities, including video cameras, for use in teaching and training programmes incorporating teacher self-evaluation and observation projects. A full-time administrator, who arranges bookings for meetings and training, and prepares resources, manages the suite. So far, the suite has hosted a wide variety of training and developmental activities. Staff have also used the space for internal training, including curriculum development, performance management, moderation of pupil work, working with trainee teachers and new staff, and meetings with each other and with external agencies.

In a large research project into professional development Hustler et al. (2003) found that most teachers worked with traditional notions of CPD (such as courses, conferences, INSET days). Developing a culture of development and enquiry has been the key to many schools' success.

As an NQI who apparently has lots of spare 'NQT cash' within school I am at a loss as to where to look for available courses. I have only been on one course and want to participate in as many as possible next term. Any suggestions as to where to look, good websites etc.?

This type of comment is so frequent! People often only think of professional development as referring to courses, yet the range of on-the-job, off-the-job, and close-to-the-job professional development opportunities is huge. Guilt at being away from the classroom, a lack of information about course quality and funding shortages are stopping many teachers from updating their subject knowledge and skills in the job (Leaton Gray, 2005). The aforementioned NQT should try to find out how much money is available and then make it go as far as possible, factoring in supply cover costs. As someone who runs lots of courses I am painfully aware that participants get charged anything from zero to £295 + VAT, and all for the same thing, though the venues and food vary. Rather than wondering what courses to go on, this NQT should approach it from the opposite angle. What does this person want to be better at or know more about and what's the best use of time and money? Courses may not be the best way: often going to see someone who has that expertise is much better because the learning will be tailor-made. What about drawing on ASTs – for free? They have a day a week for outreach work and many feel under-deployed.

The *London's Learning* CD draws an analogy between food and CPD (see Table 3.1), saying that 'the shift is from the 'supermarket' approach of one-off INSET activities undertaken by large groups of staff unrelated to individual, team or whole school needs

Table 3.1 *Food and CPD analogy*

Food	*CPD*
1. Indiscriminate selection of items of food prompted by TV advertising, two for one deals. Items rarely make a meal.	Bolt-on or one off CPD 'items' unrelated to the needs of the individual. Items rarely add up to a coherent individual development plan.
2. Items selected from a shopping list: basic plan of what is wanted.	An element of selection of CPD activities, possibly what is always chosen.
3. A recipe is used to select the food with a picture of what the items of food will look like in combination.	Needs identification leads to selection of CPD activities and the purpose of CPD is appreciated.
4. A menu of balanced courses determines the selection of food.	A coherent individual plan where needs are matched with a range of CPD opportunities.
5. A vision of 'healthy eating' determines the menu, recipes, shopping lists and items of food chosen.	A vision of CPD in which individuals and teams engage in opportunities and activities, which have an impact on both staff and pupils.

to a professional learning community in which there is an 'à la carte' vision of the purposes and principles of CPD for all staff' (DfES, 2005d: 2.1).

Teacher development doesn't just happen through the trial and error of teaching in the classroom. It has to be done effectively so that it has a positive impact and gives good value for money. The costs of going on a course, for instance, include the fees, travel, subsistence and supply cover but there are invisible costs too: the time and effort taken to analyse needs, find the right course, and to book it up. Then there is the cost of disruption to pupils' education, and to colleagues who have their timetable altered or who have to support the supply teacher. How can these costs be quantified? Against these questions of cost, however, there needs to be an analysis of benefits but how can they be measured? How do you measure what people have learned; their greater self-confidence and esteem; that new-found energy; what they do differently and its impact on the school and all their present and future pupils? Teachers can note down what they've done as a result of CPD on a sheet such as Photocopiable 6 in the Appendix.

Here are some ideas for coaching and mentoring, having learning conversations, self-study and watching Teachers' TV, observing other teachers, visiting other schools, going on courses and conferences and being observed. Let's start with coaching and mentoring.

Coaching and mentoring

As I explained in Chapter 1, the Government wants to see more coaching of teachers by teachers – and not just because it's cheap! There is, however, considerable confusion about terms and definitions around coaching and mentoring. Mentoring is mainly about helping early professional learning and brokering access to a wide range of professional learning opportunities, including coaching. Coaching focuses on the development of specific skills, knowledge and the associated repertoire of teaching and learning or leadership strategies. The circles diagram (Figure 3.1) illustrates overlapping relationships between mentoring and coaching, and the DfES outlines some other features of the roles:

Mentors should:

- develop a broad and explicit learning agreement with the person they are mentoring. This will encompass a range of topics. Processes may extend from factual briefing about basic information, through shared planning linked to observation to, at the other extreme, providing access to personal counselling;

- draw upon the wide range of skills, expertise and opportunities available locally and broker access to such resources;

- use formative assessment to support progress towards goals and set clear expectations of both partners;

- underpin progress towards self-directed learning through planned, staged and agreed withdrawal of guidance and support as professional skills and confidence grow;

- make sure that learning programmes and activities take account of the need for trust to enable professional learners to take risks;

- generate an atmosphere of trust, boundary setting, particularly in relation to assessment or accreditation, and confidentiality;

- make sure there are opportunities to learn from observing the practice of others, as well as from being observed, receiving feedback and reflecting on evidence;

- contribute to a mentoring culture that recognizes the learning benefits for mentors as well as those being mentored and builds upon these strategically;

- recognize that mentoring requires skill and experience and make sure that mentors have access to professional development opportunities both as they become mentors and as they enhance their practice on a continuing basis; consider 'mentoring and coaching' for mentors.

Coaches should:

- establish learning agreements between themselves and those they coach. These should make clear each person's expectations, and set boundaries for the relationships and the confidentiality of the information being shared;

- start with developing shared understanding of learning goals that are largely framed by the person who is being coached;

- develop coaching cycles which include shared planning for integrating new approaches into practice, learning from observation, shared interpretation of experimental, practice and/or development experiences and joint reflection on next steps;

- take turns in peer coaching, to support each other. The commitment to reciprocal learning helps to establish the trust needed for risk taking. It also makes explicit the significant learning benefits inherent in both roles (DfES, 2005c: 22).

As was noted in the previous chapter, adults learn best when they determine their own focus, through being asked questions and being given time to reflect. Those acting in the role of coach need to have the appropriate personal qualities and the knowledge and skills to be able to coach in subtle but effective ways. The power of the coaching model comes from the use of questions, rather than advice. The coach's expertise is in active listening on a number of levels, asking questions and holding the member of staff accountable for the actions agreed.

There is a lot of evidence (Cordingley et al., 2003) to suggest that acting as a mentor or coach is highly beneficial but this is not often used to help develop experienced teachers.

> Learning to be a coach or mentor may be one of the most effective ways of enabling teachers to *become* good and excellent practitioners; current practice

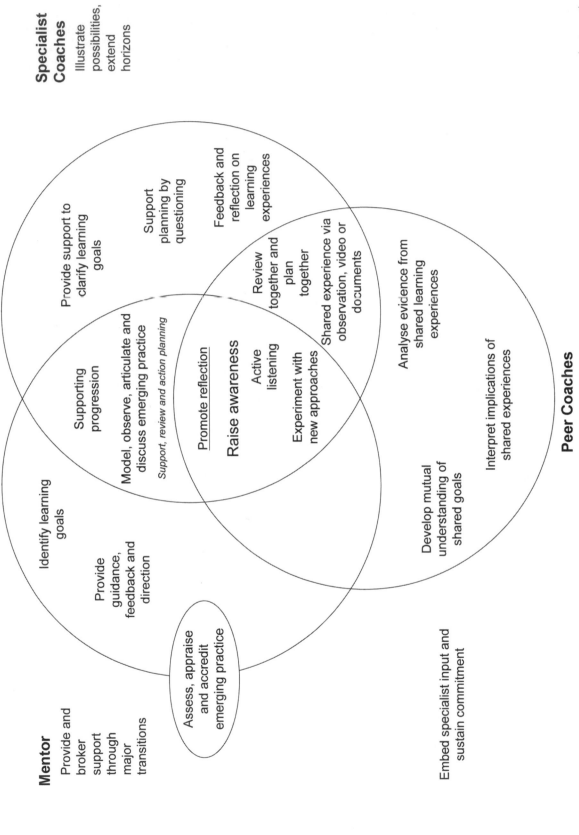

Specialist Coaches

Illustrate possibilities, extend horizons

Mentor

Provide and broker support through major transitions

Identify learning goals

Provide guidance, feedback and direction

Assess, appraise and accredit emerging practice

Supporting progression

Model, observe, articulate and discuss emerging practice

Support, review and action planning

Provide support to clarify learning goals

Support planning by questioning

Feedback and reflection on learning experiences

Promote reflection

Raise awareness

Active listening

Experiment with new approaches

Review together and plan together

Shared experience via observation, video or documents

Analyse evidence from shared learning experiences

Interpret implications of shared experiences

Develop mutual understanding of shared goals

Embed specialist input and sustain commitment

Peer Coaches

Source: Cordingley et al. (2005: 17).

Figure 3.1 *Overlapping relationships between coaching and mentoring*

appears to concentrate the opportunity amongst those who have already reached this stage. (Cordingley et al., 2005: 17)

The skills of coaching can be beneficial in the classroom with pupils too. One teacher said: 'I spent most of my time in the classroom saying "why don't you try . . ." or "the next thing you can do to improve is . . ." so to learn the skills for giving this kind of feedback to adults has made me think about the way that I work with the youngsters too'.

Box 3.1   Coaching Trios

At Mayfield School in Portsmouth, teachers are organized into cross-curricular 'coaching trios', each has colleagues with varied teaching experience: 'We don't want teachers to feel they are being assessed or inspected, which is one of the reasons why the trios are made up of teachers from different subject areas,' explains Mr Harbour. 'It's a non-threatening way of developing good practice across the curriculum.'

Coaching trios observe one another using a specific skill in the classroom. Although coaching trios meet formally during staff development sessions, many meet informally to discuss issues. For new or less-experienced teachers their coaching trio can be a vital source of support. Kerrie Paskins, a graduate teacher of English at the school, has found coaching particularly helpful. 'You can learn so much from your peers,' she says. 'It's great to listen to other peoples' ideas and it's a great confidence booster when others like your ideas. I was initially nervous about it – particularly as I had the headteacher in my trio – but it was reassuring to find he was so positive about my ideas.' (Murray, 2004)

Emotional literacy is attracting an unprecedented amount of interest in the educational world, especially on coaching and mentoring courses. It's the practice of recognizing, understanding, appropriately expressing and managing emotions in oneself and other people. It reinforces much that effective teachers have always known about the importance of the emotional state of the learner.

In helping teachers develop, coaching is about people feeling valued and supported, and providing the chance to understand their feelings. The important thing is to avoid scaring people with an overzealous introduction of 'therapy-style' sharing sessions! The ideal is for individuals to develop their own emotional literacy and gradually move on to working with colleagues, recognizing and helping them.

Teaching is emotionally draining: one has so many relationships and feels such a sense of responsibility. However, too close an emotional identification with the job damages teachers' health. When people get stressed they fall into a downward spiral towards the inability to cope both on a professional and personal level. Spotting stress in teachers you are helping is an essential skill – and also knowing how to deal with it in yourself.

When things are tough

One needs emotional literacy to deal with tricky situations, such as aggression. One can react in any of four ways:

1. *Aggressive*: giving as good as you get will make the other person angry, resentful, hurt or demoralized. The chances are that you are so well brought up that you will be hopeless at being aggressive, at least in comparison with people for whom it's a very practised art!

2. *Passive*: backing down, withdrawing, crying, running away or admitting that you're rubbish. All pretty humiliating and once the word gets around you will have more people walking all over you.

3. *Manipulative*: hints, flattery. Some people, especially Heads, are very good at this but it takes lots of skill.

4. *Assertive*: just calmly repeating the state of things as you see them.

These options are useful for you, and to recognize as strategies used by those you're trying to help. Assertive behaviour is usually the most helpful. It is the direct and honest expression of feelings and opinions that calls for respect. When you're assertive people know where they stand with you and neither you nor they should get upset. Being aggressive or passive takes a lot out of you.

 Despite having started a debating society at the school and coached them to victory in their first speaking competition, I am useless in the classroom. Pupils don't listen, so I have to repeat simple instructions. When I discipline pupils for bad behaviour, their parents phone in and say I'm picking on them. I have gone from being an infectiously happy and enthusiastic person who spent hours after school and holidays helping, coaching and broadening pupils' horizons, to a depressed and introspective saddo who feels a failure.

People in a mentoring or coaching role try to get people thinking, maybe to help with pragmatic solutions rather than perfect ones. So, for instance, someone having behaviour problems might benefit from the story about a young boy walking along the seashore after a storm. Thousands of starfish had been washed onto the beach and the tide was going out, meaning death for the starfish. The boy was picking up starfish and throwing them back into the sea. 'Why are you bothering to do that?' asked a passer by. 'You cannot possibly make a difference!' 'I made a difference to that one,' said the boy, throwing another one into the waves.

When things are tough, encourage the teacher to think of the pupils who do listen and behave and focus on teaching them. In most classes there are a few very badly behaved pupils and some well-behaved ones. Think of the rest as sheep that will follow the prevailing wind (sorry about the mixed metaphors!). Perhaps one bit of advice might be to try to focus on the goodies, ignoring the naughties as far as possible, or at least being philosophical about the chances of turning them round. That way, at least some pupils will learn something, and more 'sheep' will come on board.

Having tried everything (detention, parents, letters), I've given up on the 15 or so bad kids. I give them simple, short tasks to do (like word searches, crosswords etc.) and as long as they are reasonably quiet I leave them to it, while I get on with teaching the ones who want to learn. I now have eight who still do what they want but seven are back on track.

Learning conversations

All teachers can think of a conversation that has changed their professional practice. The GTC survey of spring 2004, based on the responses of more than 4000 teachers shows that a substantial majority gain their inspiration for their most effective lessons from talking with colleagues. Almost all (97%) say they have engaged in professional, knowledge-sharing conversations with their colleagues (see www.gtce.org.uk/Teacher-Survey04). The GTC considers that a learning conversation is a planned and systematic approach to professional dialogue.

Read the learning conversation extract in Box 3.1. This took place on the TES New Teacher Forum in March 2005. See how strangers can support each other. 'Evergreen', a trainee primary teacher, sent out a cry for help to which 'Teachur', a newly qualified secondary teacher, responded. Then the dialogue continued over several weeks. Both gained a lot of confidence from the flattering things they said to each other. Evergreen got lots of reassurance and ideas both from Teachur and the drama teacher. But how different it could have been if people had posted things like:

'Give up now! If you have problems like that they're impossible to change. You haven't got what it takes to be a teacher';

'Stop overreacting! You sound like a drama queen!';

'How awful for you';

'Don't waste your time going to a drama teacher';

'Your course director has it in for you – contact your union!'

It's useful to analyse what Teachur did – not consciously but because he's the sort of person he is. The way he makes a story out of the imagined interview with the head sounds friendly and funny. Things like 'coz you sound like a groovy chappy' entertain, amuse and flatter. Teachur is getting Evergreen on side by this chatty, funny and almost flirtatious style. He has mentored or coached in a very natural, human way. He has great credibility with her as a real teacher but not someone too distant in experience – he's only one year ahead of her. But the relationship is a reciprocal one. What do you think Teachur got out of it? Why is he spending so much time 'talking' to strangers on the internet? He clearly loves talking about teaching and learning. Like many teachers, he is driven by a desire to help people. He knows he has learned a lot and is really happy to share, but not in an 'in-your-face' way.

Box 3.2 Learning conversation: edited extract (from *TES* New Teacher Forum, March 2005)

Evergreen: After a difficult second placement, concerns have been raised about my progress on the course. If I am deemed not to have made sufficient progress, I will receive a formal written warning from the course director, which according to our trainee handbook, has to appear on a reference. I have booked a session with a drama teacher this week as my body language and presence in the classroom were one of the targets.

Teachur: Look at it this way. Let's say a job application form from you hits a HT's desk. The HT invites you to interview coz you sound like a groovy chappy to teach at his/her school. In the interview he/she asks you about your experiences on your PGCE . . . so you tell them:

> Well, I was having a few problems with the pace and tone of my speaking and with my body language/presence in the class. This was really holding me back and was not having a positive affect on my classes. So, I wanted to make sure that I tackled this. The best thing I have done, aside from lectures and talks, was spend some time with a drama teacher. I know, that might sound silly, but I learned some incredible things. I have developed the use and range in my voice (to be assertive, to be supportive, to be quick, to be slow, etc.); I have learned to use my body in a different way for different purposes, moving around lots in an energetic way, or focusing the children on a certain space; I have thought about my proximity to the children and physical boundaries. God, I learnt more in a couple of hours with that drama teacher than I think I have over the whole PGCE when it comes to my physical and vocal presence in the room.

I don't think a head teacher or interview panel EVER want to have some snotty, inexperienced nerd who puts across the 'I'm a 100% package' crap!!!! In my opinion, the best teachers are those who are willing to learn.

Evergreen: Hi Teachur, your post really cheered me up. Really looking forward to my drama lesson tomorrow. The teacher said an hour would be enough to start off with, 'cos it's really tiring! I showed her my tutor's report from the last placement and she wants a copy to work from so she knows exactly what I need to get out of the session. I just hope the HT who interviews me is as enlightened as you! And yes, I won't forget you and I will press for drama in the curriculum! I confidently predict you'll be the enlightened HT within the next 5–10 years if that's the way you want to go.

Teachur: Hi Evergreen I am somewhat too young to be a HT in the next 5–10 years! Bless ya. And thanks for your kind words. Your own confidence has appeared to grow on these forums too, which has been great to see! It's wonderful you have found a drama teacher that has taken on board your needs and is enthusiastic about your progression.

Evergreen: Went for my first drama lesson today. We talked about breathing (apparently my breath control is very good!) and I read a passage from a book. The teacher recorded it, played it back and we discussed about varying the voice: cadence etc. We talked about me as a person and the fact that although I think of myself as confident, my body language is saying otherwise! She told me about standing with feet slightly apart and body evenly balanced (says the Royal Family stand like this!) We also discussed how I 'tick': the fact I want children to like me and whether that actually matters for a good teacher. I thought this was an hour well spent and am going for more lessons, heartened by the fact that the drama teacher thinks I have the makings of a very good teacher if I can overcome these problems.

Teachur: Great to hear you got some good stuff from your 'workshop'. I totally agree with the feet thing. I refer to it as standing 'in parallel' – with the feet at about the shoulders' width apart. It is evenly balanced, allows you to move quickly and freely and promotes a feeling and image of confidence. Great to hear you've been given that tip! Also, on the 'tick' thing – even though I haven't met you I can imagine what the drama teacher is talking about. The pupils need to see you as their teacher, and will respond to you more if you are firm and fair, as well as consistent. Then you will find that they 'like' you anyway. They will like you if they feel safe and reassured, and feel like they are learning from you. More importantly, if you are someone who CARES, they will know that, and they WILL like that! And you certainly are a person who cares, and has all the other factors too! Anyhoo, great to see you felt that there's some good stuff there, and I'm sooo chuffed that someone has said to you, face to face, what a great teacher you'll make.

Evergreen: I'm still mulling over the points made at the drama session yesterday. My 'homework' for the week is to listen to myself at home and get the other members of my family to listen too. The teacher noticed that I sometimes stutter a bit at the beginning of sentences and I admitted that I sometimes interrupt someone before they've finished speaking! My family will be flagging it up if I do either of these!

Self study and Teachers' TV

Much development does not require going anywhere but having the time to read, study and think. Self-study can take many forms:

- Reflecting on progress so far;

- Learning conversations: talking to other staff about teaching and learning;

- Reading the educational press;

- Watching Teachers' TV;

- Being mentored or coached;

- Learning more about strategies for teaching pupils with special needs, those with English as an additional language, or the more gifted and talented ones;

- Visiting local education centres, museums and venues for outings;

- Looking at the educational possibilities of the local environment;

- Working with the SENCO on writing Individual Education Plans (IEPs);

- Improving subject knowledge through reading, observation, discussion and so on;

- Analysing planning systems in order to improve your own;

- Analysing marking and record-keeping systems to improve your own.

There are many materials for self-study around, especially from the national strategies – literacy, numeracy, primary and Key Stage 3. As well as good old books from the library, there are plenty of videos and DVDs. For instance, the Key Stage 3 Strategy DVD *Teaching and Learning for New Teachers in the Secondary School: Interactive Study Materials* (DfES, 2004b) is packed full of study materials. It holds the equivalent of several weighty tomes and videos on one small disk. After logging in you have to create a user profile by going through statements such as 'when designing lessons to structure learning I have a clear understanding about the nature and use of learning objectives', ticking whether you 'always', 'sometimes' or 'never' do. You then study the units in which you have identified weaknesses. These are broken down into bite-sized chunks, which is handy for people with only small slots of time.

Teachandlearn.net is an online subscription service run by The Open University and BBC. So, for example, MFL teachers can access a unit, written by a leading academic, on 'Flaubert', the geography teacher a unit on sustainable development, and so on. Each unit is driven by a guided sequence of activities, which can be carried out collaboratively with one or two colleagues, with a whole department or team or individually.

Launched in February 2004 Teachers' TV can be a great way to help teachers develop. It's on 24 hours a day on digital platforms and you can watch programmes online at www.teacherstv.tv, and download them too. But watch out – people have said it is motivating but quietly addictive.

Programmes are in short chunks of just 15 or 30 minutes and are divided into three 'zones': primary, secondary and general. They cover a whole array of topics. A primary science programme inspired Cathy Goodey, a Year 5 teacher at Princes Plain Primary in Bromley:

> I've taught electricity a couple of times with children running round a 'circuit' of other children, mimicking the particle flow. The one on TTV did it similarly but with balls being passed round. If my class could cope with the physical process of continuous passing, each child having one ball at any one time, it'd help their understanding. I'm going to try it out – but now I think about it, with an improved model for the switch!

See how the programmes reassure but spark new ideas? Teachers' TV is a great source of professional development for students, newly qualified teachers and established teachers. Cathy Goodey believes that, 'it's reassuring to see methods I've used in the classroom applauded and seeing strategies that are new to me – or ones that I'd simply forgotten'.

The trouble is that some people see Teachers' TV as 'INSET training being done on the cheap and in our own time'. This is a good point. Schools need to recognize the time that people spend watching it – and notice the benefits of this way of learning by incorporating Teachers' TV into its menu of professional development activities and arrange team discussions around a programme.

For people entering the profession, Teachers' TV is a window on the world of teaching and learning. A trainee feels that 'it's valuable to have the time to watch and reflect on other teachers' practice and consider improvements – something that I really don't get the opportunity to do on the Graduate Teacher Programme'. A secondary NQT listed many things she liked about individual programmes but concluded: 'I think what I got most out of in the programmes I watched, though, was a better understanding of kids in the classroom'.

Teaching is a solitary business. This is the real advantage of Teachers' TV: it gives people the opportunity to spy on and discuss lessons without having to intrude or disrupt. They can dismiss, damn, discuss or copy the ideas – and it's all safe.

Observing other teachers

 The absolute BEST thing observation-wise is watching another NQT teach. This is because when I observe experienced teachers it is sometimes quite depressing ('Oh God! I'm rubbish! I can never teach like this!' etc.) and it seems impossible to raise your standards to match the amazing things you see.

Whatever role people have and whatever stage they are at they will learn a great deal about their job from watching others doing it. Similarly the more people watch children learning, and think about the problems that they have, the better their teaching will be. Newly qualified teachers find it the most useful of all induction activities (Totterdell et al., 2002). Here is a selection of things for teachers to observe and do:

- other teachers teaching: advanced skills teachers, supply teachers, experienced, inexperienced . . . anyone!
- teachers in other schools, similar and different to yours;
- someone else teaching your class;
- someone else teaching a lesson that you have planned;
- how pupils of different ages learn and are taught;
- discussing lesson observations;
- team/partnership teaching;
- tracking a pupil for a day to see teaching through their eyes;
- a colleague take an assembly;
- a visiting expert;
- shadowing a colleague;

- learning walks: strolling round your own and other schools;

- visiting and seeing other schools in action;

- working with an artist in residence.

Effective teachers make the most of any opportunities to observe others, formally or just informally around the school. They watch a range of people. It is very cheering to see that everyone has similar problems and it is fascinating to study the different ways people manage them. Peer observation is stressful, so in a sense things get worse before they get better, but it is worth getting over initial discomfort, reluctance and shyness about being observed and sharing problems with colleagues.

However, observing so that one gets something out of it is not easy. People need to have a focus for observation because there is so much to see that they can end up getting overwhelmed. Observations need to be linked to something that people want to develop. For instance, someone who wants to improve pace in introductions needs to notice the speed of the exposition, how many pupils answer questions and how the teacher manages to move them on, how instructions are given, resources distributed, and how off-task behaviour is dealt with. Teachers can note down what they see and how they could integrate it into their own practice, using a sheet such as Photocopiable 7.

Diana had problems with behaviour management, so observed a teacher with a good reputation for control. She gained some ideas, but found that much of this experienced teacher's control was 'invisible': he just cleared his throat and the class became quiet. So she observed a supply teacher and someone with only a little more experience than herself. It was hard to persuade them to let her observe, but when they realized how fruitful the experience and the discussions afterwards would be they accepted. These lessons, though not so perfectly controlled, gave Diana much more to think about and she learned a range of useful strategies. Both teachers found it useful to have Diana's views on the lesson, as a non-threatening observer, so they too gained from the experience.

 When you're given feedback, it's sometimes hard to identify exactly how to implement the suggestions. For instance, I was told a few times that I needed to give my lessons more pace – which I fully accepted – but I wasn't able really to work out how to do this, or which parts of my lessons weren't pacy enough. It was only when I saw an NQT in my own subject teach a lesson that I got what they meant about pace because she was too slow too.

When observing, it's essential to look at teaching in relation to learning. Why are the pupils behaving as they are? The cause is usually related to teaching. People should be encouraged to jot down things of interest, certain phrases that teachers use to get attention, ways they organize tidying-up time and so on. Forms with prompts can help observers focus by writing a few bullet points about what they have learned, and the ideas that could be implemented. It is valuable for staff to log who they have observed.

England's General Teaching Council (GTC) is promoting the value of peer observation. It says,

> As the *observer*, it can give you the opportunity to:
>
> - watch and understand the development of complex classroom interactions;
> - observe in a structured way how, when and with what effect a teacher uses different strategies;
> - investigate the different effects of a range of teaching styles and strategies on how pupils respond and learn;
> - internalize new approaches you may see in others' practice so that they become part of your repertoire;
> - connect knowledge and practice.
>
> As the *observed*, it can give you the opportunity to:
>
> - unpack the complexity of what you do in the classroom so that you can develop and pass it on;
> - look closely into one particular aspect of your teaching (e.g. questioning techniques);
> - experiment with new teaching strategies;
> - focus on what is happening to the learning of a particular group of pupils;
> - discuss your teaching style(s) in a non-judgemental environment;
> - connect knowledge and practice. (2004: 4)

At Brislington School, mentors and trainees video their lessons to reflect on together. These videos enable the mentor to give a running commentary of the motivations that influenced externally observable decisions through the course of the lesson. When the mentor has modelled this process of reflecting out loud, the trainee is then supported to do the same thing with a video of their lesson. One surprising spin-off has been the power of watching the videos of lessons and discussing them with the pupils involved (GTC, 2004).

Teaching a lesson with someone else can be a great way to help teachers develop. At Grange Technology College in Bradford up to a third of teachers work at partnership teaching every year (Barnard, 2005). Partnership teaching was developed by Deane Narayn-Lee and his department to shift away from the traditional model of supporting pupils with language difficulties at the back of the class but it has spread throughout the school. The double-act nature of partnership teaching is reflected in the planning: the two teachers prepare their lessons closely together in Monday morning brainstorming sessions. A typical lesson might see Mr Narayn-Lee introduce the topic, bringing out important terms, phrases and ideas, then handing over to the subject teacher to discuss the practical side. Then it's back to Mr Narayn-Lee who might stimulate a discussion, before finishing with pupils producing some writing. The teachers encourage each other to be more imaginative, to push the boat out.

Visiting other schools

 It's good when teachers share good practice and work out for themselves what is needed. It was a lot more helpful than an INSET as the needs for each school can be catered for on an individual basis.

It's great to go on a 'learning walk' around a classroom or school. It is different from evaluations and is the least threatening approach to introduce visiting into the school culture. The London Challenge Leadership Visits programme enables newly appointed heads, deputies, senior and middle leaders to spend up to three days in schools in a similar context as their own in order to view good practice and encourage the cross-fertilization of ideas and expertise that comes from collaboration. New leaders are asked to say what they would like to get out of the visits and then the programme manager identifies a host school that has a recognized degree of expertise or success in the area of interest with a similar context. Then the visit is set up and people are provided with personal action plans, formal evaluation and feedback tools for people to make the best use of time.

The model of sharing school experience at key career points appears to be a very useful and specific form of professional development for leaders: 'I can honestly say it was ten times better than any INSET day I have ever been on, and I am 100% sold to the idea of learning from successful schools' (Earley et al., 2005: 50). This description from a visit by a new head of PE gives a sense of how visits are organized:

> I was given an introduction to the team and their backgrounds, a tour of the school and facilities; and time with the Head of Department to ask questions and talk about what goes on on the 'ground floor'. I was given a presentation on assessment, monitoring and tracking . . . I was also given a wealth of information about various things . . . It was a great day and the HoD has suggested that they become our 'critical friend'. We have been in contact via email and information has gone in both directions. (Earley et al., 2005: 50)

Since visits are tailor-made, individuals feel a sense of autonomy and ownership, something that has been highlighted as a vital component in the evaluation of the national early professional development pilots (Moor et al., 2005). Schools seem to like playing host and they appear to gain as much from the process as the visitors. A head, talking about her teachers who hosted several visits, said: 'Explaining how they worked made them question and clarify our practice and underlying philosophy. Teachers can be great self-doubters so having the time to talk to someone openly and honestly is very affirming' (Earley et al., 2005: 50). Far from reinforcing the status quo, people have found visiting similar schools interesting and empowering: 'It was very inspiring for me. The school is in a similar situation to my school and showed some parallels to the problems we face, such as facilities'.

Courses and conferences

With the swing towards in-house professional learning there is also a danger that courses and conferences could be like the babies thrown out with the bathwater. When well chosen, going on a course is one of the ways to gain a good level of professional development very quickly. As one teacher said: 'even the weakest courses give you something to think about and develop but when the training is good it can move your thinking and practice forward considerably' (Boyle et al., 2003). There are hundreds of courses run by LEAs, subject associations, national bodies, teacher associations and unions, private sector providers, universities, private outfits and schools themselves. Conferences offer the chance to hear an inspirational speaker and meet up with other people with the same interest. They are a good way to keep informed of the latest developments in the field.

Some courses and conferences are held after school, on Saturdays or during holidays, which means that pupils' learning is not disrupted. Not many people seem to know that teachers can get paid to attend courses in their own time – after all, they are saving the school the cost of a supply teacher or the hassle of covering absence internally. Here is what it says in school teachers' pay and conditions:

> Relevant bodies should decide which CPD activities teachers may be paid for and set an appropriate level of payment, bearing in mind that all payments should be funded from money saved on supply cover . . . However, where possible, training courses should be scheduled during the five non-teaching days during which teachers are required to be available for work, or out of hours, to minimize the disruption caused to pupils' education caused by teachers' absence from the classroom. Payments to full-time classroom teachers should only be made in respect of those activities undertaken outside the 1265 hours of directed time. (DfES, 2003: 30)

The opportunity to network with other teachers and broaden horizons is an important factor in deciding where to go on a course. LEA courses enable teachers to meet up with people from local schools and get to know the advisers and inspectors, which is hugely advantageous. Sometimes the local scene gets a little insular so going to a venue that attracts a wider range of people can be great and give a broader perspective. This is also a good way to find out more about other schools, albeit at third hand.

One of the big advantages of going on a course is that actually being out of the school building and atmosphere gives people some time and space to think, to reflect. However, there's a danger that people might be inspired by what they see on that day, but then they come back into school and by five past nine they are overwhelmed by the minutiae of what goes on in the classroom. Jenny Reeves (2005) says teachers need a third space, a temporal or physical place where they can work out how to implement the new things that they have learned.

Some courses that last for more than one day have activities built into them so that people are forced to 'learn/do/review'. For instance, within my four-day accredited induction tutor course participants are asked to discuss Transition Point 2 with their

NQTs, set up an individualized induction programme, set and review objectives and related action plans for the NQTs' development through the year; write feedback from lessons that they have observed; and write assessment reports at the end of each term. All these are tasks that induction tutors have a statutory responsibility to do but being on the course means that people get a chance to discuss them – and be rewarded through gaining 30 credits towards a Graduate Diploma.

Teachers – almost by definition – like learning. Some will be keen to improve their tennis, are adult education groupies and a few like some rigorous intellectual stimulation. They get fed up with one-day professional development sessions, especially when so many of these reflect the school's or the government's agenda and not theirs! They want something meatier – an MA, which usually takes one year full time to complete or two years part time.

 I have found the MA fantastic for expanding my educational philosophy and knowledge – you will get to know the relevant policies etc very well and there is a massive world of research and writing that I did not even know existed before I did it.

There are increasingly convincing arguments and evidence about how much teachers develop through doing action research in their schools. Research-informed practice enhances teacher self-efficacy and professionalism and brings about change in schools for the benefit of teaching and learning.

Being observed

To get the most from being observation, people need to think about what they'd like to get out of it. Feedback on teaching is really valuable – and normally very boosting. Research on induction found that NQTs found being observed and receiving feedback on lessons as useful as observing other teachers. The views of this NQT were typical: 'It's vital. It's just so informative having someone watch you teach because you can't see everything and sometimes you don't see what you do well, as well as the things you need to develop' (Bubb et al., 2002: 139). Being observed was indeed considered 'the most nerve wracking part but I think it's the most effective'. Many spoke of it as a positive and constructive experience. One NQT said that she 'loved' being observed: 'I love showing my kids off as well . . . I choose my lowest sets . . . It raises their own self-esteem and it makes me feel really proud of them.'

There is, however, limited use in one-off observations. While they are useful in tracking professional development to meet identified targets, they are a one-stage process with limited impact unless there are follow-up observations by the same person to provide some insight into a teacher's development. Having watched *Teaching with Bayley: Too Much Talk* where John Bayley is seen coaching a teacher through a series of lessons, teachers in a focus group organized by the Institute of Education at the University of London said: 'We have people coming in and observing us . . . but when the feedback is given, fine, for that particular topic, but nobody has ever come back to that lesson again to see if the feedback is implemented' (Collins and Burn, 2005: 7).

Table 3.2 *Concerns about being observed*

Your concern	Possible solutions
Pupils will be passive – won't engage	Plan something to get them lively. Use talk partners ('turn to your neighbour and tell them the answer to my question').
The behaviour of one child will ruin everything	Plan for an assistant to be with the child. Make sure the work is just right. Send them to someone else during the observation.
I can't get or keep attention	Do your best; plan well with this in mind; have as much written on the board beforehand as possible.
The pupils play up when I'm observed	Tell them that they are being observed. Remind them that you are expecting exemplary behaviour.
Technology will go wrong	Set it up beforehand; check and double check; have a back up in case it does go wrong.
I'll forget or lose key resources	Make a list of what you need, tick items off when collected, organize them.
The teaching assistant won't turn up	Keep reminding them that you're relying on them and give them a plan of what they should do.
The pupils will finish work too early	Have some extension work; make the task harder or open ended.
I'll forget what I planned to do	Do a clear written plan – that very act helps lodge it in your mind; keep your plan to hand on a distinctive clipboard to avoid it getting lost; have a spare just in case you leave it somewhere; use prompt cards; rehearse the lesson structure in your mind.
I'll forget what to say	Script key parts of the lesson especially questions; rehearse out loud and in your head.
I'll let the class wander off the point	Stay focussed; put timings on your plan; write up the learning objective; plan questions that will guide the pupils' thinking.

Coping with nerves

Most teachers don't like being observed and get nervous. Being nervous is perfectly normal, and people can tell when you are and make allowances. One way of helping people to cope with nerves is to understand why they get worried, then they can do something about it, as illustrated in Table 3.2.

My first OfSTED observation was with a wonderful Year 11 class who were very well behaved. However, the problem came where the second activity (music – a listening worksheet) came, and one of the students said to me: 'we've already done this'. I had photocopied the wrong sheet! Thirty minutes to go, lesson plan up the Swanee, no resources!

Here are some suggestions for how to prepare for an observation:

- Plan with even more care than usual. Be completely prepared;

- Have a copy of the lesson plan for the observer;

- Be absolutely clear about what you want the pupils to learn and do;

- Make sure your teaching and the activities match the objectives;

- Have as much stuff as you can written up on the board beforehand;

- Think about what the person observing you is looking for. Address things that have not gone well before;

- Do everything you can to feel confident: wear your favourite teaching clothes; encourage others to boost you; sleep well; tell yourself that you are going to teach well;

- Don't panic if things start to go wrong! Think on your feet. Most teachers have some lessons that go swimmingly, others that are okay and the occasional disasters. There are a huge number of factors to do with you and what you are teaching and then a whole heap to do with different classes, what lesson they have just had and what time of day it is. So, don't beat yourself up about it.

 I had spent the lunchtime writing stuff on the board only to discover when I got into the classroom that the class teacher had rubbed it off because she thought it wasn't important and wanted to give me a clean board. I had to re-write the stuff as the kids came in. After I had used the board I went to rub the writing out so I could do something else ... except it wouldn't rub out because she had used baby lotion. Luckily I had a flip chart in the room so I went to use the flipchart to find that there were no clean sheets of paper. At this point my mentor was laughing, as were the kids so I just had to laugh and run with it.

The dialogue that takes place after a lesson observation is vital, as is illustrated in the *Teaching with Bayley* programmes on Teachers' TV. Use it to discuss the minutiae of the lesson and to get ideas for improvements. There is no such thing as a perfect teacher (except in your mind) so lessons don't have to be perfect, but teachers do need to show that they are reflective, making progress and acting on advice. If the lesson doesn't go well, teachers should see this as an event to be learned from and given advice on. It was a one-off performance, a snapshot, and things *can* be different tomorrow. Be open to ideas, accept and even encourage constructive criticism. This has its painful side but handled well, it's worth it.

In the next chapter we look at how to observe teachers, a key activity for anyone helping them develop.

4

Observation

There's a great deal more observation of teaching than ever before, carried out by a range of people: inspectors, headteachers, members of senior leadership teams, subject leaders, induction tutors, mentors, teacher tutors and governors. There are also more teachers watching others in order to improve their own practice. With the short notice inspection system, senior staff are watching lessons so often that some teachers are refusing to let trainees observe their classroom practice. Teaching unions have called for a halt to the observation overload. They say excessive scrutiny is damaging teachers' morale and confidence. Chris Keates, general secretary of the National Association of Schoolmasters and Union of Women Teachers, said: 'In some schools observation is a euphemism for destructive, punitive and excessive monitoring, often carried out by those least in touch with the realities of the classroom' (Slater et al., 2005: 1). Observation needs to be done well – and be helpful to teachers.

With development in mind, this chapter offers concrete ideas about how to go about observing teachers and considers the difficult area of written feedback and monitoring – putting pen to paper.

Issues

Observation is a powerful tool for assessing and monitoring a teacher's progress. Used well, it can also be a way to support teachers, because observation gives such a detailed picture and enables very specific objectives to be set. Observing someone teach gives a really detailed picture and is an opportunity to stimulate some really useful reflection on teaching and learning. A headteacher of a large secondary school is convinced of its value:

> I have seen an increase in staff confidence. At first staff were unsure of how being observed would impact on them and it may have been considered

45

threatening, but with a good dialogue and feedback, it has proven to be very valuable and they are now able to understand how this sort of CPD, carried out by staff within the school, has enhanced their classroom skills (personal communication).

As noted before, research shows that newly qualified teachers find it the most useful of all professional development activities (Bubb et al., 2002).

The value of observation, however, depends on how well it is planned, executed and discussed afterwards – and how knowledgeable and astute the observer is. Few people have had any in-depth training in how to observe or even to discuss what effective teaching and learning is. Yet both are crucial if observers are to feel secure in their judgements, and the observed to feel that it is a valid exercise. Importantly, observation takes time and money, both of which need to be spent well. An observation takes about three hours:

- Thirty minutes to plan it with the teacher and prepare for it;

- One hour to observe and make notes;

- One hour to reflect and write up a summary;

- Thirty minutes for the post-observation discussion.

Be aware that your presence in the room, however unobtrusive, will have some influence on what happens in the room: pupils may behave better, the teacher may be more inhibited than usual. As Hal Portner (2003: 45) says: 'When you observe a class, you actually observe a class being observed'. It is almost always a stressful experience, not only for the teacher but also for the observer. The fewer observations a teacher receives, the greater the pressure for them to go well so they need to be conducted fairly. The observer may also find observing stressful, because they feel inexperienced and uncertain of the best way to go about it. The year group and area of the curriculum to be taught may not be familiar. They may feel that the quality of their observation and feedback will compare unfavourably to that of others. If they are the person responsible for the teacher they will also be mindful of the need to move them forward while maintaining a good relationship. This can lead to misplaced kindness. Teachers sometimes feel that they are not being sufficiently challenged, and that the observation and feedback is only superficial. This is particularly true of the most successful teachers, but they too need to be helped to develop professionally.

 Is there an agreed limit on the number of times a teacher can be formally observed in one academic year? I am not an NQT nor am I subject to capability procedures but I've been observed six times in two terms. I have heard that the head can 'drop in' at any time he/she chooses but are there limits on the number of times he can send his 'henchSMT' around our department? By the way, nobody ever gets written feedback or any follow-up to these visits.

Observation and giving feedback are very complex skills, which need training and practice. The important thing to remember is that the whole process needs to be seen in the context of raising pupil achievement, and thus it needs to be useful for the teacher. To this end consider the context of the observation: the stage the teacher is at; how they are feeling; their previous experiences of being observed; the observer's relationship with the teacher; the time in the school year, week and day of the observation; and the disposition of the class.

Observers also need to recognize their own values, beliefs and moods. When I was less experienced I had strong views on what I considered good teaching to be. With hindsight, this was very subjective, narrow and arrogant. This is why it is important to concentrate on the progress the pupils make before judging the effectiveness of the teaching, and to avoid preconceptions about the teacher. The more I observe other people, the more convinced I am that there is no one best way to teach.

 Rarely a week goes past without someone coming in to watch me, requiring detailed lesson planning and a one-hour meeting after school to feed back.

Some schools see trainees and NQTs as guinea pigs to practise their observation and feedback skills on, which is not fair. It can be really damaging to have your every move analysed. Some people have been over-observed and that has put them under a lot of pressure. One NQT was observed 12 times in nine weeks: 'I feel like I'm in goldfish bowl'. Three people watched him at the same time on one occasion: the head, deputy and a consultant who was also an OfSTED inspector. Stressful or what!

Mandi, a new teacher, was upset: 'I got an unsatisfactory rating on my first observation'. Should people who observe use OfSTED gradings? This is unhelpful, unnecessary and may even be inaccurate – is the person a trained inspector? Mandi was told her lesson was unsatisfactory because a small number of pupils were off-task and did not produce good enough work. In fact, it is amazing that at this stage in her career only a small number of pupils did not work hard enough! She was worried about the consequences of getting the 'unsatisfactory' rating, when the only impact of this should have been that the school gave more targeted support to enable her to succeed.

This sort of experience will knock any teacher's confidence, which is a crazy thing to do – nobody can teach without heaps of it. It would be much more helpful for the observer to talk about strengths, successes, small improvements and areas for development. Obviously there are going to be many things new teachers could improve on but there should be discussion about what to prioritize.

Bad practice in observing causes great problems and can damage teachers' confidence. I've heard of situations where the observer:

- arrived late and disrupted the lesson;

- observed without any notice;

- corrected the teacher's errors in front of pupils;

- looked bored or disapproving and even fell asleep;
- did not give any feedback;
- gave written feedback without an opportunity for discussion;
- contradicted the views of previous observers;
- gave simplistic feedback without any ideas for further development;
- made erroneous judgements based on poor knowledge of the context;
- upset the teacher without giving positive ways forward.

It's helpful for the people who make observations to get some feedback. Do ask whether the observations you make are helpful! To build up trust, arrange for the teacher to observe you before you watch them.

As with many areas, it is useful to have a policy on procedures and good practice before, during and after an observation. The rest of this chapter will provide some things to think about.

> **Activity 4.1   Observing a lesson**
>
> Get hold of the free Teacher Training Agency pack, *Supporting Assessment for the Award of Qualified Teacher Status: Secondary English*, publication no. 99/2-00. This came out in 2000 to support teacher training so there is likely to be a copy in the school. It consists of a video and a booklet. Watch English teacher, Juliet, teach a lesson on autobiography to a Year 7 class. Teachers of any phase or subject will be able to gain a great deal from watching it.

Good practice in setting up an observation

Plan when the observation is to take place and how long it will last. A whole lesson is ideal but is not always necessary, depending on the focus. Around a week's notice seems fair for all concerned. Choose a lesson that the teacher feels happy with and that will give you the information you need. If you want to get a rounded picture of the teacher try to observe a lesson at a time of the day and week that has not been covered before. If teachers keep a simple record (such as the one in Table 4.1) of when they've been observed, you can see gaps at a glance. There's so much difference between how one functions in the morning and later in the day!

> Complaining that you are being observed at an inappropriate time or that you have been given little warning simply allows the Head to argue that you are insecure about your practice.

While your diaries are out, agree a time and place to discuss the lesson, giving both of you time to reflect. Ideally, feed back at the end of the day or at most within 24 hours of the observation. Give the teacher a written copy of the arrangements.

Table 4.1 *Record of lessons observed*:* observations of Oliver's teaching 2004–5 as NQT

Date	Time	Class	Subject	Observer and position
27 Sept 04	9.30–10.30	Y3	Literacy	Induction tutor
3 Nov 04	9.30–10.30	Y3	Literacy	Literacy coordinator
18 Jan 05	11.00–12.00	Y3	Numeracy	Induction tutor
2 Mar 05	11.00–12.00	Y3	Science	Science coordinator
19 May 05	11.00–12.00	Y3	Science	Headteacher
13 June 05	1.30–2.30	Y3	Art	Induction tutor
27 Sept 05	11.00–12.00	Y3	Science	Science coordinator
2 March 06	11.00–12.00	Y3	Numeracy	LEA adviser

*See photocopiable 4 for a blank version.

Agree a *focus* – ideally something the teacher is trying to get better at. This will not exclude you from noticing and commenting on other things but will ensure that you have information on the key area that you are working on. In all cases, it should be linked to helping pupils learn more effectively.

Clarify *purpose* – why are you observing? Is it for appraisal or professional development? Let teachers have a copy of the proforma and the criteria you will be judging them by. What will happen to the observation notes you make: will they be given to a third party or not? What happens if you have grave concerns about aspects of the lesson? Will the quality of teaching and learning be graded? This is not necessary and can cause problems but if it is, observers should be trained to do this accurately.

OfSTED (2002) found that a quarter of the schools coupled lesson observations for performance management purposes with those for curriculum monitoring. This meant that teachers did not always have a clear understanding of the aspects on which they should focus and the observers did not necessarily carry them out with an appropriate degree of rigour. There was often insufficient clarity about how a lesson observation for performance management purposes might differ from one for curriculum monitoring, how the focus might relate to the teacher's objectives, and what the outcomes might be in terms of influencing the teacher's further professional development activities.

Discuss *ground rules* such as how your presence is to be explained to the class, what you are going to do, where you should sit, and your exact time of arrival. Discuss what you will need before or at the beginning of the observation, such as the lesson plan and access to the planning file. If you need something in advance, agree when the teacher is going to give it to you.

Proformas

It is good practice to let teachers have a copy of the proforma and the criteria you will be judging them by – but what are you going to write on it? There's no such thing as an ideal lesson observation format, yet sometimes anything seems better than a blank piece of paper. Different formats will be useful at different times and for different situations but they should be appropriate to the purpose and focus – certainly I believe that inspection forms should only be used for inspection! See Table 4.2 for a summary of the advantages and disadvantages of formats. There are ones that require very little writing, because you just tick boxes but although that makes things easy for the observer these forms are no good for the teacher who will want to know why one box was ticked rather than another. Some people recommend event sampling where you note down what is happening every five minutes or so. These types of notes are useful for observing an individual child but are pretty impossible to use in a classroom. Other people write a running record of what happens in a lesson with a few ideas dotted around like a stream of consciousness, but I guess a video will do that as well. And be mindful of the fact that different formats might lead you to write different things.

Table 4.2 *Formats for lesson observation: advantages and disadvantages*

Format	Advantages	Disadvantages
A sheet with teaching prompts	Enables you to write about what seems most useful, but the prompts focus you on areas you need to consider.	Depends on the skill and experience of the observer to pick out useful bits and make suggestions.
Strengths and areas for development sheet	Gives a clear picture of your judgements because it just focuses on strengths and areas for development.	Needs to be backed up with evidence and examples. Best used as a summary sheet after the format above has been used.
Inspection evidence form	Good emphasis on relationship between teaching and pupil response and learning. The grading useful in judging teaching and learning.	These may seem too formal and their association not conducive to how the observer wants to be perceived. Hard to use if not familiar with the inspection criteria.
Participant observation – teach while observing	Reduces the stress on the teacher. Should benefit the pupils in that lesson.	Hard to participate and observe. You are not simply judging the teacher's work but your own too. Can undermine the teacher's authority.
Observing without making notes	Being released from the need to write enables the observer to see a great deal. Reduces the stress on the teacher.	Without the structure of some note making the observer can end up seeing everything and nothing. Can be idiosyncratic and lack evidence.
Diary description	Gives lots of detail that the teacher may be unaware of. This should ensure objectivity.	Observer writes reams – much of it not particularly useful. A video can describe the lesson objectively, but only an observer can analyse.

Table 4.2 *Continued*

Format	Advantages	Disadvantages
Running record with judgements and tips	Judgements in context, which gives a clear picture with reasons for the teacher. Allows flexibility in writing about the things of most import	Involves lots of writing. Depends on the skill and experience of the observer to pick out useful bits and make suggestions
Timed event sampling	Might give a good description of what went on in a lesson. Useful for tracking an individual pupil or seeing the lesson through their eyes.	Involves lots of writing and not useful for giving the big picture. Observer might miss something because it doesn't happen at the right time. Best used when observing one child.
Lesson structure	Useful for seeing the effectiveness of different parts of a lesson.	May not give a big picture. Can give too much emphasis on the structure rather than teaching and learning.
Form with sections under headings	Keeps you focused on commenting on key areas that you can decide on before the lesson.	The size of boxes may constrain, or make you feel that you are writing something for the sake of it.
Checklist – statements to be ticked or commented on	Easy for the observer to complete. Gives a big picture.	No flavour of the particular lesson. No examples. Doesn't give reasons for the judgements.
List of action points	Clear what to improve.	Depressing list of things to do without any recognition of successes.

There are two ways of writing down notes from an observation:

1. notes you make during the lesson;

2. a summary of strengths and areas for development for feedback.

I think both should be used. That way the observer can make informal jottings during the lesson, knowing that they will be summarized in a tidy product.

Thus, my personal preference is for the format shown in lesson observations 1a and b, which I designed to suit most types of lessons. Let me explain why. When I'm observing I need to concentrate on what is happening rather than trying to answer questions or fill in boxes so I need a copy of the teacher's lesson plan and a blank piece of paper to write down what seems to me to be important. I don't write too much about the structure of the lesson – I scribble bits on the copy of the lesson plan for this, using ticks, noting down times that certain things happened and making the occasional comment ('nice idea', 'kids fidgeting'). However, there's a danger that I might only notice what's in my face. That's where the prompts come in: glancing down them reminds me to make a judgement on the quality of the plan, the ground rules, the teacher's voice or whatever. Even if I don't get time in the lesson to write about these points in detail I will make a jotting or give it a tick, cross, question mark or exclamation mark.

I use lesson observation 1a (Table 4.3) as a jotting sheet, just for me knowing that my notes will be pulled together in a tidy summary afterwards. The version here is nice and tidy but in real life it will be full of abbreviations, quotations of what was actually said, and unfinished statements and with awful handwriting and grammar! If the teacher wants to see what I have written that's fine but the format of lesson observation 1b (Table 4.4) is what I want to share with them. On this sheet I spend time reflecting on what is significant in the lesson, writing the strengths and successes liberally before I see the teacher and thinking about what I think might be areas for development. I keep these in my head rather than commit them to paper because it is important for me to know

Table 4.3 *Lesson observation 1a – Prompt sheet for note making in the classroom**

Teacher:	Juliet	Year Group:	Y7 23 pupils
Additional adult:	Yvette, support teacher	Set: Low	14 EAL, 2 statemented and 12 other SEN
Subject:	English: structure of autobiography and past tense	Date and period:	1.40–2.36 p.m. 14 March
Prompts	Comments and evidence. What impact does teaching have on pupils?		
Planning ✓ Groundrules ✓ Behaviour man ✓	Pupils come in calmly and settle down – clearly know expected behaviour. Good to have Yvette go through homework straight away while you get your things organized.		
Expectations ✓✓ Organization ✓ Resources ✓ Learning objectives? Subject knowledge ✓ Explanations ✓ Tg strategies? Voice ✓ Pace ✓ Questioning ✓ Motivating ✓	Wonderful snappy start. Lovely smile – real warmth that the pupils react well to. Good to ask the difference between biography and autobiography, though you didn't pick up on the boys' use of the term 'story' which would have been useful. I don't think you shared learning objectives or told the class the big picture of the lesson. These things really help pupils cue into what you want them to do and aids their learning. It's also school policy. I like the way you hook the children's interest by asking them whose autobiography they'd like to read. It does however take a while. Could you use talk partners to make even more of this part of the lesson? Very good choice of text – appealing to all boys and girls. A good hook – shows you have thought about what will motivate the pupils. Good,		

Table 4.3 *Continued*

Differentiation? *Additional adults?* *Feedback* ✓ *Activities* ✓*?* *Plenary?*	snappy getting of the chapter headings from a range of pupils – again perhaps you could do some pair work for this to get more out of more of them. Ordering was done efficiently and democratically, but to get where you want. Lovely humour and lively style, in getting them to articulate why they know it's David Beckham's autobiography. Good use of Yvette to read paragraph. How could she be more involved at other times? Good changing of tenses as a class, and coping with errors. Lovely to get the class to clap the boy for reading aloud – really celebratory and boosting. The pupils seemed to cope well with the activity of writing out a paragraph in a different tense. It would have been brilliant if there'd been a purpose for doing so. Could you have differentiated this to challenge pupils more? It was good to get them working though they had little time to do so (five mins?). Could they have done more individual/paired work throughout the lesson? You told them what to do for homework: finish off drafts. Shame there wasn't a plenary to pull together what they've learned. What did they learn? What did you expect them to? Pupils packed up and left sensibly. Time: 1.50 Pupils on task: all; off task: 0. Time: 2.15 Pupils on task: all; off task: some looking a bit switched off.

*See Photocopiable 2 for a blank version.
Source: Bubb (2003: 134).

what the teacher thought of the lesson. Some things are easier to approach orally or in an oblique way.

During the observation

Go in with a positive frame of mind: ineffective teaching is rare so get ready to spot the good stuff! This may sound obvious and patronizing but I have known so many teachers who almost automatically look for things to criticize, things that they would have done better. It is essential to look at teaching in relation to learning. One must always be thinking about cause and effect. Why are the pupils behaving as they are? The cause is often related to teaching. Thus, the observer needs to look carefully at what both the teacher and the pupils are doing. Too often the teacher gets most of the attention, yet the product of their work is the pupils' learning – the proof of the pudding.

Be as unobtrusive as possible but remember that your very presence is affecting the lesson. Like a science experiment your presence in the room is a variable. If the teacher has not given you a place to sit, choose one which is outside the direct line of the teacher's vision, but where you can see the pupils and what the teacher is doing. At the side, half way down is best. When the pupils are doing activities, move around to

Table 4.4 *Lesson observation 1b – Summary of lesson observation**

Strengths of the lesson

Well done, Juliet, this was a lesson that I enjoyed. You have so many talents as a teacher! In particular the strengths of this lesson were:

- Your clear enjoyment of teaching and self-confidence
- Strong voice, good intonation – clear explanations
- Warmth towards the pupils – your smile, eye contact, facial expressions and body language all work to encourage and give pupils the confidence to take risks. Very positive feedback and use of praise to boost self-confidence
- Good questioning esp stretching EAL pupils to explain what they mean
- Excellent control – all the above help in this area but you are also very confident yourself and this helps. You expect them to behave in a certain way, and they do. You handle the odd misbehaviour briskly with a change of tone ('don't call out, Michael') and good use of body language (turning away, not giving attention) but then you catch Michael being good – brilliant!
- Well resourced and organized
- Clear plan, with timings
- Good use made of the OHP
- Good use of support teacher at start of lesson and in reading out a paragraph to emphasize the tense difference.
- Good choice of text that motivates and is part of their culture

Areas for further development

Try to increase the learning of more of the pupils more of the time, for example:

- Share learning obj – WALT & WILF?
- Big picture of the lesson
- More paired work: discussing whose autobiography they'd like to read, writing and maybe ordering chapter headings
- Having a plenary for them and you to evaluate learning and progress
- Make even more use of support teacher

Objectives

Plan lessons to increase the learning of more of the pupils more of the time.

Teacher's comment

This was helpful – thanks
Signatures: Juliet Coley, Sara Bubb

---

*See Photocopiable 3 for a blank version.
Source: Bubb (2003: 135).

ascertain the effectiveness of the teacher's explanation, organization and choice of task. Look at different groups (girls and boys; high, average and low attainers; and pupils with English as an additional language or special needs) to see whether everyone's needs are being met. Ask things like, 'Sorry, what did Miss ask you to do?' and 'What are you learning? Why?'.

Box 4.1   Minimizing Intrusion when observing

South Dartmoor Community College uses a system called Sound Assist. 'It's basically an earpiece and a microphone,' says PE teacher and teacher training mentor Jason Trevarthen. 'It's a two-way audio system between the mentor and the student that allows for immediate feedback.' In PE it means that a trainee can be taking a lesson on one side of the school field, while at the same time being coached on teaching technique by an experienced teacher, who could be 50 metres away. 'There are lots of benefits: I can offer advice when things are going badly, and give encouragement when things are going well.' This instant feedback speeds up learning.

Dene Magna School has two observation rooms where people can watch other teachers and use the two-way audio system. A storeroom has been converted into an observation suite equipped with video equipment connected to cameras in the classrooms, allowing lessons to be watched and filmed. Using two-way mirrors, the observers can watch the class without the pupils realizing. (Based on Revell, 2005a)

Read the lesson plan, paying particular attention to the learning objective. Is it a sensible objective, and do the pupils understand it? It is useful to annotate the plan, showing what parts went well, when pace slowed, and so forth. Look at the teacher's planning file and pupils' work to see what the lesson is building on.

Make notes about what actually happens (with significant timings), focusing on the agreed areas but keeping your eyes open to everything. Make clear judgements as you gather evidence. Refer to the criteria you agreed to use – have a copy with you.

Try to tell 'the story' of the lesson, by noting causes and effect. For instance, what was it about the teacher's delivery that caused pupils' rapt attention or fidgeting? Think about the pupils' learning and what it is about the teaching that is helping or hindering it. Note what pupils actually achieve. Teachers are not always aware that some pupils have only managed to write the date and that others have exceeded expectations.

Avoid teaching the pupils yourself or interfering in any way. This is very tempting! Pupils will often expect you to help them but once you help one others will ask. This will distract you from your central purpose, which is to observe the teaching and learning. It is not wise to intervene in controlling the class unless things get out of hand, because it can undermine the teacher's confidence and may confuse the pupils, who will see you as the one in charge rather than their teacher. As far as possible be unobtrusive.

Remember that your presence will normally have an effect on the pupils – if you are an established member of staff they will often be better behaved but sometimes show off. It is sometimes useful to leave the room for a few minutes and loiter nearby to see if the noise level rises when you are not there and to get a feel for the atmosphere as you go back in. This can also be used when the lesson is going badly because it gives the teacher the opportunity to pull the class together.

Look friendly and positive throughout, even (and especially) if things are not going well. Say something positive to the teacher as you leave the class. The teacher will be very anxious, and will almost always think the worst unless reassured. Ideally, give an indication that you were pleased with what you saw but if that's not possible be empathetic – 'you must have the patience of a saint!' or 'understanding fractions is so hard'.

After the lesson

 I have been officially observed by the PGCE course manager and been told it was an atrocious lesson!! Thing is though, I had no idea it was that bad! I have been told that I need to establish myself more as a teacher, be more authoritative and more enthusiastic about my subject.

Views differ about what should happen after an observation. Montgomery, for instance, says: 'It is really important for the debriefing interview to take place immediately . . . Lessons, lunches and days should not be allowed to intervene' (2002: 54). I disagree. Even if there is time, don't fall into the trap of discussing the lesson straight away because you need to think about the teaching and learning you have seen, focusing on strengths, what has got better and one or two areas for development. Be clear about your main message – this will take some thinking about. There is no point listing every little thing that could have been better: there will always be something, since there's no such thing as a perfect lesson.

You need to have 'the big picture' in your mind in order to convey it to the teacher. Remember, it should be useful to them – aim to help them develop. You want to avoid the extremes of crushing them or giving the impression that things are better than they really are. It is a very fine line to tread, but your knowledge of the context and the teacher will help you.

Attend to the physical setting of the discussion. Choose a place where you won't be disturbed – you never know how someone is going to react. Even when the lesson has gone well, teachers can become emotional because, if nothing else, they are very tired! Providing a drink and a bite to eat is a nice caring touch and can oil the wheels of your discussion. Position chairs at right angles for the most conducive atmosphere. This enables you to have eye contact but not in the formal direct way that sitting opposite someone across a desk would ensure. Mind you, sometimes you might want to choose such a formal setting to get a tough message across. Sitting next to someone is awkward because it can be hard to get eye contact or to move away.

I don't like the term, 'feedback', as it suggests that the observer is going to do all the talking and the teacher will sit and listen, passively. Thus, what should happen after a lesson observation is a 'discussion'. People develop by thinking and coming to solutions themselves rather than being told what to do and criticized.

 I have been teaching for about a year and a half, and have always had positive lesson observations. Today, a member of middle management picked up on everything that was negative, and gave no positive feedback. I was told the lesson was too slow (even though others have said pace is good); that the kids were bored and uninvolved, although they were on task and had met the aims of the lessons by the end; that I wasn't marking the work properly, I wasn't praising enough (which I always do!); that my classroom is the wrong size; and my TV was too small.

Try to ask questions to guide the teacher's thinking, but not in a way that intimidates or implies criticism. Encourage reflection and listen well by asking open-ended questions, such as:

- How do you think the lesson went?

- What were you most pleased with? Why?

- What were you trying to achieve?

- What did the pupils learn? What did the lower/higher attaining pupils learn?

- Why do you think the lesson went the way it did?

- Why did you choose that activity?

- Were there any surprises?

- When you did . . . the pupils reacted by . . . Why do you think that happened?

- Help me understand what you took into account when you were planning.

- If you taught that lesson again, what, if anything, would you do differently?

- What will you do in the follow-up lesson?

Avoid talking about yourself or other teachers you have seen unless you think this might be useful to the teacher. Comments such as 'I wouldn't have done that' or 'I would have . . .' are inappropriate and can irritate and alienate the teacher. It is sometimes tempting to talk about your most awful lesson. This can be comforting for the teacher, but can detract from the purpose of the discussion. Aim for the teacher to do most of the talking and thinking.

Paraphrase and summarize what the teacher says. This helps you concentrate on what is being said and is very helpful in getting a clear shared understanding of what the teacher thinks. It involves reflecting back your interpretation of what you have heard, which can be very useful for the teacher. Use phrases such as 'So what you mean is . . .', 'In other words . . .'.

Be aware of your body language and notice the teacher's. A large proportion of communication is non-verbal. Also, watch what you say, and how you say it. Focus on the teaching and learning that took place, using specific examples of what pupils said and did. Be positive throughout. Be sensitive to how the teacher is taking your feedback, and ease off if necessary: Rome wasn't built in a day. There will be other opportunities for raising points, perhaps through subtle hints in the staffroom.

Good post-observation discussion is:

- *Helpful* – aiding the teacher, rather than making the observer feel good or superior;

- *Prompt* – takes place at the end of the day after the lesson observation;

- *Accurate* –based on specific observations/evidence;

- *Balanced* – the positive emphasized and points for development related to the focus chosen as an objective;

- *Respectful* to the teacher's perspective – allows for input from the teacher;

- *Related to objectives* set for review and directly actionable by the teacher;

- *Conducted* in a quiet and private space.

Take Paul's maths lesson as an example. He is a secondary trained teacher who taught for three years in secondary schools before moving to primary where he has been teaching for five years. He is well established in the school, is confident, popular with staff, parents and pupils, and likes helping colleagues, especially with ICT and science. The observer, however, had some concerns about his maths lesson and Box 4.2 shows what she wrote.

Box 4.2   Observation on Paul's maths lesson

Years 3 and 4 middle set. Maths LO: to explore, visualize and construct cubes

The maths lesson was a new unit on shape. Lesson plan was very detailed and three pages long – almost a script. Paul shared the learning objectives at the start of the lesson but used exactly the words written on the plan: 'to explore, visualize and construct cubes'. He did not attempt to explain what they meant or what the children would be able to do or understand by the end of the lesson. The children I spoke to didn't understand. The lesson was really an investigation on ways to make nets of cubes to see which way of arranging the squares would work. Well organized and resourced.

The lesson started with a test, which did not seem appropriate. Paul asked questions and children individually had to write the answer on a white board and then mark each other's. Some questions were very hard, such as 'what is a nine-sided shape called?' He asked: 'what is a four-sided shape called?' but he was looking for the term quadrilateral rather than square and rectangle. He made no attempt to notice who was getting answers right and who was getting them wrong. A fair number of children found it hard, which was worrying for a little introductory activity.

His expectations were high, perhaps too high. For instance, he started talking about congruent shapes which confused the children and wasn't pertinent to the learning objective. Explanations were clear and fairly well scaffolded. He had excellent control and a good level of mutual respect.

Questioning was weak. Almost all the questions were closed. He only chose people with their hands up and predominantly chose boys. At one point he asked eight boys, and only one girl. His voice dominated the lesson: he missed opportunities to get children explaining ideas. There was no differentiation written on the plan or apparent to me as an observer. Perhaps since it was a set, Paul thinks there is no need for differentiation.

Table 4.5 *The strengths and weaknesses of Paul's lesson*

Strengths	Weaknesses
• Very detailed plan	• Learning objective not understood by children.
• Well organized and resourced	• Activity didn't match the LO.
• Explanations clear	• Test was an inappropriate way to start and made
• Excellent control	some children anxious – too hard
• Enthusiastic	• Questioning
• Mutual respect	• No differentiation
• High expectations	• Missed opportunities for learning
• Practical – drawing and making nets	

So, there were a great many concerns! Rather than give Paul the notes as they are, I think it would be helpful to list strengths and weaknesses or things that are a concern (Table 4.5). When you look at the strengths you can see that they are really significant and need to be clearly conveyed and celebrated. Of the weaknesses, which do you think are the ones that are most significant or from which other issues could be covered? Choose the biggest hitter – the one that's going to make biggest difference to all subsequent lessons. Imagine the six weaknesses as roads you could go down. Avoid ones that are cul de sacs: the ones that Paul will argue with. For instance, he may disagree with you over whether the test was inappropriate or too hard – he knows the children better than you – so that's not the best route to take. Similarly, he could argue that there was differentiation by outcome in the task which was a reasonably open-ended investigation. You would be on surer ground with the issue of the learning objective not being clear and not exactly matched to the activity, because you have evidence from the children. It's a good road to go down and one that will have a significant impact on teaching and learning.

Framework for a post-observation discussion

It is useful to have some sort of structure for the post-lesson observation discussion or professional dialogue – a learning conversation. You need to use time well, feel in control of the situation and know where you want to get. A common feedback structure is shown in Table 4.6. However, the style of this structure – telling someone their strengths and then areas for development – tends towards the teacher being passive, listening to what the observer has to say. The teacher doesn't pay attention to the strengths because they are waiting for the 'but'. This is not always the best way to encourage someone to develop professionally. Your aim should be to encourage the teacher to play a more active part and engage in a dialogue.

Malderez and Bodoczky (1999) suggest using a framework for feedback that has different styles and actions in each of the phases. I have adapted their framework (see Table 4.7) to address issues and areas for development first (which lead into setting

Table 4.6 *Typical feedback structure*

Phase	Commentary
1. Observer asks teacher, 'How do you think the lesson went?'	Teacher doesn't know what the observer's judgement is, so may be cagey. Some teachers say little ('It was ok') and others say too much. Some people go off on a tangent that after 10 minutes leaves you utterly confused.
Observer either: • goes over their notes chronologically with strengths and weaknesses mingled;	• This gives a detailed picture of the lesson, but overall may not give a clear message about what was good and what needs to be improved;
• outlines strengths and then areas to develop;	• Strengths and areas for development are clear, but the teacher may not pay attention to what you liked because they are waiting for the 'but', the negatives. In both these cases the teacher is inclined to be passive while you feedback unless you ask questions.
• 'So I think these are your action points';	• This gives the teacher no active role in deciding what needs to be worked on. They may act on your suggestions successfully but often they won't.
• 'What do you think you need to work on?'	• This gives the teacher some choice in prioritizing what the observer thinks they need to do, but responsibility is minimal.

Source: Bubb and Hoare (2001: 69).

objectives) and to end by discussing the teacher's strengths. I have found that this helps the observer stay focused on the main points because it stops one going round in circles or going off on unhelpful tangents. This is how the phases work.

Pre-phase 1: Decide on key points

It is important to go into a post-observation discussion with a clear view of the teacher's strengths, and what you think they need to work on to be even more effective. Make a list of any 'weaknesses' of the lesson. Don't fall into the trap of criticizing because you wouldn't have taught it like that – you didn't. Identify ones that impacted on the pupils' progress and well-being. This should stop you raising points that are simply based on your own idiosyncratic feelings. For instance, some people will feel irritated by things such as the teacher pacing up and down, punctuating every sentence with 'er', or speaking in a monotone but these should not be raised unless they are affecting pupils' learning. You should also consider whether the teacher would be able to change or improve – things like voice and mannerisms are very hard to alter and strike at the very heart of a person.

Table 4.7 *Improved framework for a post-observation discussion*

Phase	Commentary
Pre-phase 1. Decide on key points	Have a clear view of the teacher's strengths. List them on the summary sheet. Make a private list of the 'weaknesses' of the lesson. Prioritize – which ones impacted most on the pupils' progress and wellbeing. This should stop you raising points that simply come from your own idiosyncratic feelings. For instance, some people will feel irritated by things such as the teacher punctuating every sentence with 'er', but only raise issues that affect learning. Consider what the teacher will be able to change or improve.
1. Warm up	Thank the teacher for letting you observe. Give a headline of what you thought of the lesson. This is what they want to know. If it went well, say so. If it went badly say something reassuring, commenting on the pupils ('What a handful') or the subject matter of the lesson ('fractions are so hard'), but that does not mislead them.
2. Teacher's views	Ask the teacher how they thought it went. Some will think the lesson successful when you had misgivings, but more often people focus on the things that didn't go well. Either way, you have an insight into how they think which will determine how you develop the feedback. If they think they are better than you think they are, consider their reasoning – they might be right. If, after listening, you really feel their needs are even greater than you originally thought be tougher and clearer in your message. If they are overly self-critical, you need to boost them up.
3. Areas to develop	Address the weaknesses that the teacher has identified or ones that you consider. Link these to the effects they are having on the pupils. A useful strategy is to use factual statements about what you heard or saw, without including a judgement: 'Your introduction took 40 minutes'; 'I saw three pupils yawn during the plenary'. This allows the teacher to consider why. Probe further, asking questions, such as 'Do you think that was time well spent?'; 'Why do you think that is?' that guide the teacher to think more deeply. Discuss alternatives: 'How else might you . . .?' See your role as someone who allows teachers to reflect off; who asks the questions that encourage them to think of solutions. Note down areas for development. Perhaps phrase them as objectives: what should happen, with what help and by when.
4. Strengths and successes	Having got areas for development out of the way you can now have a relaxed and thorough discussion about the teacher's strengths and the successes of the lesson in terms of pupils' learning. This will make the teacher feel boosted and confident, and ready to implement the areas for development, though there is no need to mention them again. Don't be afraid to use fulsome praise, linking teaching to the progress and well being of the pupils.

Phase 1: Warm up

Thank the teacher for letting you observe. Give a brief headline of what you thought of the lesson – this is what they want to know so if it went well say so. If it went badly say something reassuring or sympathetic, commenting on the children ('what a lively group') or the subject matter of the lesson for instance ('fractions are so hard to teach'), but do not mislead them.

Phase 2: Teacher's views

Ask the teacher how they thought it went, and why. This will give you an insight into how they evaluate their work. If they have exactly the same view of the lesson as you, things are easy. Others will think the lesson successful when you had misgivings, but more often people focus on the things that didn't go well. Either way, this gives you an insight into how they think and this will determine how you develop the discussion. If they think they are better than you think they are, consider their reasoning – they might be right. If, after listening, you really feel that their needs are even greater than you originally thought be tougher and clearer in your message. If they are overly self-critical, you need to boost them so forget about raising negatives for now. Most teachers say something like: 'Well, I was quite pleased with the lesson overall but I wish . . .'. This naturally leads to a discussion of an area for development.

Phase 3: Areas to develop

Having gained more information from the teacher, you need to decide quickly on the most important things to address. Link these to the effects they are having on the pupils. A useful strategy is to use factual statements about what you heard or saw, without including a judgement. So, if you think the pace was rather slow in the plenary you could say: 'I saw three children yawn during the plenary'. The teacher can offer a reason for the behaviour – and probably solutions. These might be any of the following:

- 'Yes, I agree. I think the way I do plenaries – asking a group to read out their work – is a bit boring.'

- 'Hmm, I think I ran out of steam by then.'

- 'Yes, those three were up late watching the football match on TV.'

However, if you interpret what was seen – 'I saw three children looking bored' – you may actually be wrong. Even if your interpretation is right, the teacher is immediately put on the defensive and is unlikely to open up and reflect in a confident way.

Probe – why?

You will need to probe further, asking questions that guide the teacher's thinking more deeply about the issue. If they come to a straightforward reason that you agree with you can move to the next phase: thinking about alternatives. Probing questions will occur to you *in situ* but generally they will be 'why' ones such as: 'why do you think that is?' You can then move into the 'how' phase.

Alternatives – how else?

When you are in this phase the teacher and you should be discussing alternatives: how to make a specific aspect of their teaching more effective. A key question would be: 'how else might you . . .?'. See your role as being someone who allows the teacher to reflect off and who asks the questions that encourage them to think of the solutions themselves. Ideally the teacher should think up their own solutions, but you can suggest some too.

Objectives

If appropriate, you can then raise the status of the discussion by phrasing action points as written objectives. Think of what things should happen, by whom, with what help and by when. Alternatively this could happen later, when there's more time and after some more reflection.

Phase 4: Strengths and successes

Having got the areas for development out of the way you can now have a relaxed discussion about their strengths and the successes of the lesson. Allow a decent amount of time for this – at least five minutes if the total discussion lasts 15 or 20. Actually, I wouldn't discuss so much as tell because any discussion is likely to revert to negatives again. This is a time for the teacher to sit back and listen, basking in your praise. This is bound to make them feel uncomfortable but persist as it will make the teacher feel boosted and confident. Don't spoil this by mentioning the areas for development again. Use fulsome praise, linking their teaching to the progress and well being of the children.

This structure takes practice, which it is useful to do in a role-play situation (see Activity 4.2).

Activity 4.2   Role-play a post-observation discussion

People work in threes, taking turns to be the teacher, the observer and someone watching the discussion. The watcher uses Table 4.8 (page 64) to note down what things happened in each phase of the discussion. You will all need to watch a video of some teaching. Try to get hold of the TTA video of Juliet, the English teacher that the observation notes in Lesson observation 1a: were written about (see also Tables 4.3 and 4.4 pages 52 and 54). The TTA booklets contain the plans, evaluations and work relating to the lessons. This gives the role-play group plenty of information to work with.

To give people experience of the different situations in which they might find themselves in discussing lessons, in each of the three role-plays the teacher responds differently to the question: 'How do you think the lesson went?'

■ *First role-play* – The teacher is reflective and open. When asked how she thought the lesson went, she says she dominated too much.

■ *Second role-play* – The teacher is very hard on herself and thinks she's taught an awful lesson.

■ *Third role-play* – The teacher thinks she has taught an excellent lesson in which everyone met their learning objective and made progress.

Each role-play should take about 15 minutes and be followed by comments from the watcher and then a brief discussion. The whole activity should take one hour.

Table 4.8 *Watcher's notes for framework for a post-observation discussion*

Phase	Commentary
Pre-phase 1. Decide on key points	
1. Warm up	
2. Teacher's views	
3. Areas to develop	
4. Strengths and successes	

People with whom I have used the improved framework feel that they were more active, reflective and boosted by the emphasis on their strengths at the end of the discussion. It also seems to take a shorter time than other feedback structures, because there is a tighter focus.

Written observation feedback

Putting pen to paper is something that everyone worries about, and understandably so. When something is written down it becomes permanent and the meanings that readers interpret from it are out of your hands so one needs to absolutely clear – and this can be difficult. It is so much easier to raise issues orally because one can use body language, expression and check understanding during an interaction. In writing there are just the words – and they can seem very stark! In this section I shall discuss the pros and cons of different formats and analyse some real written feedback to illustrate some techniques and phrases to use – and ones to avoid.

Most people would agree that written feedback should contain:

■ Praise;

■ Acknowledgement of success;

■ Identification of strengths;

■ Identification of an area to develop;

■ Ideas for improvement.

There are several sorts of comments in observation feedback:

1. *Descriptive* – what happens but without any evaluation. Some lesson observation notes are purely descriptive, saying things like 'teacher showed me the plan', but with no judgement. This is not helpful;

2. *Evaluative* – judging: 'very well planned'; 'shouting simply raises the noise and emotional level';

3. *Advisory* – suggestions: 'Dean and Wayne might behave better if they were separated';

4. *Questioning/reflective* – there are two sorts of questions:
   (a) those designed to stimulate thought and get people thinking about an area that could be improved, for example 'How could you have avoided the arguments over pencils?'
   (b) Genuine questions for clarification, for example, 'Why are you ignoring Paul's behaviour?' There isn't often a need to ask a genuine question.

Activity 4.3   Textual analysis of an observation

Photocopy observations in this chapter and underline phrases that are
   Descriptive – D
   Evaluative – E
   Questioning – Q(a) for ones that encourage reflection or Q(b) for genuine ones
   Advisory – A
What can you learn from this?

Take care over what you write

Read lesson observation 2 (Box 4.3, below). This was written as part of a visit on behalf of the LEA to quality assure induction provision and to judge whether the school's view of the NQT was accurate. It contains numerous spelling and grammatical errors (that I have drawn attention to in brackets), which is embarrassing as the person who wrote it is not only representing the LEA but is an advanced skills teacher. How would you feed back to her on the quality of her work? What do you think of it? Will it help the new teacher develop? Does it give a clear picture of strengths and areas for development? What message does it send the induction tutor in the school about the standard of lesson observation expected?

Box 4.3 Lesson observation 2: AST's observation of a NQT in Year 1

Strengths

Objectives were communicated both visually and verbally. You demonstrated through (*thorough*) knowledge of the subject and materials were appropriate for the lesson, e.g. books of the seasons and appropriate vocabulary was displayed and used (*grammar*). You made the lesson more assessable (*accessible*) by using 'Harry', the puppet. You drew upon children's previous experiences as the children were able to chant out the days of the weeks and you encouraged children to assist 'Harry' to rearrange the days in the correct order. You used a variety of activities to engage your class. You involved all the children by listening to them and responding appropriately.

You praised your class by asking them to give themselves a clap when they had achieved the correct order of the days. Generally you managed to address poor behaviour and on several occasion(*s*) you took prompt action however there was a few children who were not noticed for their actions (*grammar and clumsy phrasing*). All children were on task and knew exactly what they had to do and you had differentiated the work sheet appropriately. Your teaching assistances (*assistants*) were well informed and had personal plans as an aid to support their individual groups. You made effective use of the time available especially the countdown to end of lesson.

Areas for further development:

- Although you had work by the computer it was not switched on.

- In future you should provide a lesson plan for any lesson observations.

- Try to be more consistent: are the children allowed to call out or not?

Would you agree that the spelling and grammatical errors are so serious that they devalue what the AST is trying to say – as well as her credibility as an excellent teacher? I definitely think so but if we look beyond them to the content of what she is saying, we get a picture of a reasonable lesson although there is too little detail to be sure of what strengths the teacher has. One presumes that statements like: 'Objectives were communicated both visually and verbally' are positive but more adjectives alongside the description would let us know more. Crucially, we want to know what effect this had on the children: were they clear about exactly what they were learning and why?

Looking at the areas for further development, are we clear what the observer means? Does it really matter that the computer wasn't switched on? Maybe it did if children were expected to use it and didn't know how to turn it on but otherwise it could seem nit-picky. All areas for development should be identified as such because of their impact on pupils' progress. The second point, about providing a copy of the lesson plan for the observer isn't an area for development so this is not really the place to make such a comment. That could be raised verbally or written as an aside or in parentheses: 'Thank you for letting me observe. A copy of your plan would have helped (something to remember for next time)'. The last area for development is a significant issue so it needs to come first and be elaborated upon. The use of a question is a good technique here, and likely to go down better than saying 'Don't let people call out'.

Prompts based on the structure of the lesson (Table 4.9)

A proforma with prompts based on the structure of the lesson is useful when you have been very specific in helping teachers develop certain aspects, and want to see how they are doing in response to your input. Lesson Observation 3 has been completed using the same video of Juliet the English teacher that I used in Lesson Observation 1a. For instance, if you have been working on the start of lessons these questions will be very pertinent:

- How do the students enter the classroom?

- What is there for them to do immediately?

From these questions we can infer that the observer or whoever designed the sheet has been encouraging the teacher to work on the entry of pupils to the classroom and starter activities as calming and focusing strategies. There is a useful emphasis on the pupils but some prompts are not very useful, such as 'how long does the introduction last?' I don't know how long they should last. Is the duration important, or the quality? You could alter prompts to address areas you have been working on with teachers, removing aspects that are hard to understand, such as 'Is the learning "chunked"?'

One of the downsides to using this type of format is that it pushes the observer to write only about the things listed. There may be other striking points you might like to note but there is no room. There is also a fair amount of reading of prompts that will slow you down until you become familiar with them. How helpful will it be to the teacher reading it? Very, if they look at this form carefully since they will know precisely what you are looking for; but it could be a little like teaching to the test. If there are positive things to say in response to each of the prompts will the lesson overall be successful? Will the pupils have learned anything? That's what matters!

Writing against the QTS standards

If you are observing someone in order to give them a view on how they are meeting specific standards it is useful to have a format that makes this clear. Lesson Observation 4 (Table 4.10) is structured around the headings of the standards. The benefits of this are obvious – it forces the observer to look out for things, some of which one wouldn't necessarily note down. The downside is that there are 40 or so QTS standards to read.

The first section, Professional Values and Practice (based on the GTC code for all teachers in England), is really key but can get neglected because of the overwhelming attention given to planning, behaviour management and assessment. The first standard says that teachers must have 'high expectations of all pupils; respect their social, cultural, linguistic, religious and ethnic backgrounds; and are committed to raising their educational achievement' (TTA, 2003a). How do you demonstrate that? Well, it is in everything most teachers do: what they expect of pupils and what they let them get away with. However, some teachers allow children to call out, chat, chew gum, cuss each

Table 4.9 Lesson Observation 3: Proforma with prompts based on the structure of the lesson – using a video (TTA, 2000) of a lesson

Teacher: Juliet	*Year Group:* 7	*Number of pupils:* 23
Support teacher: Yvette		*Set:* Low	14 EAL, 2 statemented and 12 other SEN
English: structure of autobiography and past tense		*Date and Period:*	1.40–2.36 p.m. 14 March

BEGINNING

How do the students enter the classroom? What is there for them to do immediately? *Pupils come in calmly and settle down – clearly know expected behaviour. Good to have Yvette go through homework straight away while you get your things organized.*

Does the teacher greet the class positively and use praise throughout the lesson? *Wonderful snappy start. Lovely smile – real warmth that the students react well to.*

How is the lesson linked to previous learning? *Good to ask the difference between biography and autobiography, though you didn't pick up on the boy's use of the term 'story' which would have been useful.*

Is it made clear what students will learn/achieve by the end of the lesson? *I don't think you shared learning objectives or told the class the big picture of the lesson. These things really help students cue into what you want them to do and aids their learning. It's also school policy.*

How long does the introduction last? Does it refer to prior learning? *Yes*

MIDDLE

Is there a brisk/differing sense of pace in the lesson? *Good, snappy getting of the chapter headings from a range of students – again perhaps you could do some pair work for this to get more out of them. Ordering was done efficiently and democratically.*

How does the teacher cater for different learning styles? *Visual and auditory, not kinaesthetic*

Is the learning 'chunked'? *Not really, but lovely humour and lively style, in getting them to articulate why they know it's David Beckham's autobiography.*

Are students encouraged to raise questions and search for solutions? *No – this is a fairly teacher-led lesson*

To what extent do the questions/activities help student to learn? *They did but there were missed opportunities to get pupils more actively involved in learning.*

In what ways did the lesson engage the students' emotions? *I like the way you hook the children's interest by asking them whose autobiography they'd like to read. It does however take a while. Could you use talk partners to make even more of this part of the lesson?*

Are the students motivated and engaged? *Yes, most of the time. Very good choice of text – probably appealing to all boys and girls. A good hook – shows you have thought about what will motivate the students.*

Do they persist when things get difficult? *Nothing very difficult.*

How do the tasks relate to the lesson's key learning points? *I'm not sure what it was.*

Does the teacher recognize and respond to individual needs? *I couldn't see this.*

How do the students demonstrate their new learning? *Not sure there was much new learning.*

How does homework develop active and creative learning? *Good to have got the pupils to write their memories for homework.*

Does the teacher deal promptly and effectively with negative behaviour? *You handle the odd misbehaviour briskly with a change of tone ('Don't call out, Michael') and good use of body language (turning away, not giving attention) but then you catch Michael being good – brilliant!*

How are support staff used? *Good use of Yvette to read paragraph. How could she be more involved at other times?*

END OF LESSON

How does the teacher review what has been taught, has been learned and understood? *Shame there wasn't a plenary to pull together what they've learned. What did they learn? What did you expect them to?*

How is the lesson summarized and reinforced at the end? *You told them what to do for homework – finish off drafts.*

Are students encouraged to review their learning? *No Students packed up and left sensibly.*

69

other and swear. In a Year 10 English class I observed, nothing was said about the students writing in felt tip pen and doodling in their exercise books. In a Year 9 class nothing happened to the boy who got out of his seat, went over to four girls who weren't being noisy and shouted: 'Shut the f*** up!' In many classes I see pupils being praised and rewarded for producing work that they know is not good.

Teachers also have to demonstrate and promote the positive values, attitudes and behaviour that you expect from your pupils. There are plenty of shining examples of this: where the resources are well organized, clean and well presented, and displays are fantastic. This lifts the spirits of all the pupils and adults in the room – you can see them all doing their best. Other teachers' rooms are a mess. Some teachers nag at pupils about uniform when they look, quite frankly, scruffy themselves.

How do teachers speak to pupils? One young and attractive teacher peppers all her interactions with secondary students – but not colleagues, thankfully – with 'sweetheart' and 'love'. It just doesn't seem appropriate when she uses such terms of endearment with Year 10 boys. At the other extreme another teacher continually addresses her Year 2 children harshly using their full names – 'Jill Thomas'. These issues are not easy to address but having a standard to hang them on makes it easier to distance the criticism, making it less personal.

Judging excellence

Lesson Observation 5 (Table 4.11) was written during the assessment of an advanced skills teacher. Note how it's written *about* rather than *to* the teacher, which is appropriate since the audience is not the teacher herself but to contribute to an evidence base for the assessment (see Chapter 6). Do you think the teacher shows an excellent ability in teaching, managing pupils and maintaining discipline? Look at the AST standards in Chapter 6. Do you think the teacher observed meets the standards? There are certainly plenty of superlatives and the word 'excellent' is used frequently. This is something to remember for people who are going for excellent or advanced skills teacher status. Any monitoring of them should be using adjectives like excellent, wonderful, inspiring. If they aren't then either the teacher is not good enough to go for ETS or AST, or the people monitoring are not being sufficiently accurate and celebratory.

If you're helping someone to reach standards of excellence, consider how you can move them from being good or very good to outstanding. Also, encourage them to think how they can address any standards for which there is insufficient evidence.

Writing about lessons that are less than satisfactory

 We have a teacher with big control problems but instead of looking at what she's doing, she blames the children and the parents. No amount of support makes much of a difference to her.

Writing about lessons that are less than satisfactory is hard. When you're trying to develop a teacher who is not very effective, there needs to be a balance between praise

Table 4.10 *Lesson Observation 4: Writing against the standards for qualified teacher status –*
Literacy Year 1*

Professional Values and Practice
Demonstrated caring and respectful approach to all class members, work expected was
challenging but appropriate to their levels of development. Excellent behaviour management
strategies observed. Worked hard to include all children especially those with poor levels of
concentration.

Knowledge and understanding
Learning objective followed the NLS guidance for Year 1 and although it is a difficult concept for
Year 1 (headings for non-fiction books) and needed some explanation the introduction was
handled competently. S made clear effectively how she intended to progress from the LO in
subsequent lessons towards creating an end product for each child (their personal non-fiction
booklet). A range of strategies was seen to maintain good behaviour and a peaceful learning
environment.

Teaching – planning, expectations and targets
Learning objective was in line with the NLS and matched the lesson plan. High expectation of
pupils and the ability to keep children on task resulted in good standards. The TA was used to
support the learning in all phases of the lesson, worked with one of the differentiated groups and
contributes to the planning.

Teaching – monitoring and assessment
S constantly observed and questioned pupils to assess understanding – demonstrating a sound
connection with the processes of learning. Positive and encouraging feedback frequently given.
Practice of checking each group before starting to ensure the task was understood was very
effective practice. Plenary used to consolidate and check understanding.

Teaching and class management
Well-structured lesson demonstrating effective whole-class and small-group teaching. Timing and
pace was crisp without being mechanical; plenary consolidated LO, praised individual efforts and
looked forward to the next literacy lesson. The classroom is well organized and labelled; tidy with
thoughtful arrangement of the furniture and good displays. Children have easy access to
resources and during transitions organized themselves quickly and efficiently.

Further comments
S is a talented and effective teacher. She has a strong voice with clear diction and can give
explanations and instructions accurately using appropriate vocabulary. Her behaviour
management is very good, thus providing the children with clear, firm boundaries and a safe
environment in which to learn. Her weaknesses in relation to her profession therefore are related
largely to youthful inexperience.

Targets
1. To develop listening and speaking skills in her pupils
2. To improve pupils' concentration
3. To develop own awareness of KS1 vocabulary development and usage

*See Photocopiable 5 for a blank version.

Table 4.11 *Lesson Observation 5: Assessment for advanced skills teacher status*

Subject: English year group: Y7 (25 mixed ability)

Context and description of the lesson	Within a very well-planned sequence of lessons on figurative language, pupils study similes through an initial whole-class activity, which is predominantly oral before moving to individual written tasks which are matched to ability with three levels of work. Excellent planning, very clear, shared key objective with suitably differentiated work enabling all pupils to make very good progress in understanding of similes. Excellent quality of resources (including large photographs for use in whole-class part of lesson and well designed activity sheets with good illustrations for individual work – high level of teacher's own ICT skills evident here). Excellent level of expectation on this, the last lesson of the term; very good use of time and highly effective sharing session at the close to confirm good levels of understanding. Teacher very alert to full range of ability both orally, in questions, and in design of printed resources.
Teaching	Excellent, brisk opening to lesson – gets everyone 'on their toes'; quick fire questions speedily establish understanding and recognition of similes. Excellent challenge and expectation, guiding pupils away from cliché towards imaginative, original responses; encouraging experimentation with language. Very effective link to previous literacy study; excellent methodology. Excellent use of visual stimuli – develops response across all abilities (no print barrier); engages high level of pupil interest and promotes language development. Excellent use of 'Black Adder' similes – brings lovely element of humour into the lesson – higher attaining pupils see the bizarre quality! Excellent involvement of one pupil who has brought in boxing gloves to illustrate similes. Teacher very skilfully differentiates questions. Excellent design and match of printed materials assures very good progress by all. Further supported by very good one-to-one assistance during individual work. Teacher focuses her interventions very well. Excellent close to the lesson as pupils share their work and together clarify their understanding of the images. Thorough marking of pupils' work evident in exercise books.
How pupils respond to the teaching including progress, attitudes and behaviour	Pupils of all abilities, boys and girls, are well motivated: they respond positively to the teacher's high expectations. Excellent concentration, both when listening and responding during whole-class part of lesson and when working alone. Very good self-discipline, sorting out how they will record their responses. All remain on task throughout; excellent work habits evident in class and exercise books. All keen to do well. Some take handwriting books to work on during the holiday.
Attainment	High – excellent progress over time and in this lesson.
Other significant evidence	Limited space in classroom but teacher still achieves a good range of different groupings within the lesson. Excellent use of ICT in the design of resources. Excellent level of expectation in setting of holiday homework to which pupils respond very positively.

and boosting for what is going well, but also clarity about what needs improvement. The trouble is that with a less effective teacher it is hard to find positive things to say and it can be hard to diagnose which of the many problems will be the key one to address. Sometimes problems lie with people senior to you:

 It's a difficult school and we now have a new Head. Everyone is waiting for her to 'do' something radical and get going but she hasn't done anything that seems effective since September. Now the school is falling apart around me. It's really breaking my heart. Shall I say something?

Teachers' egos are very fragile, by and large, no matter how experienced they are and how big and strong they seem. Most of us are highly critical of our performance and don't need anyone else to labour over weaknesses. A hint, an idea of what could have been better, an apposite question will be enough to make most teachers scurry away, shed some tears and improve.

The comments about the maths lesson in a special school (Table 4.12, Lesson Observation 6) seem to have a good balance between positive points and ideas for improvement. There is a lot to praise, and the observer has noticed and appreciated it. This might seem an obvious point but too often good things aren't celebrated enough. Criticisms of the maths lesson are precise but subtly and kindly put, and backed up with hard evidence, as can be seen in these comments around the use of time:

> You planned for the introduction to last for five minutes, and it actually took four minutes for X to give out all the bottles. While it is good for him to be engaged in such 'helpful' behaviours, the time taken to hand out resources resulted in many of the pupils losing a degree of attention.

This style is a good way to get a difficult message across, and to give the teacher food for thought. The level of detail suggests that the observer knows the pupils and what is best for them. It would be hard to argue with the points raised because they are so linked to the effect of teaching on learning.

Most teachers will benefit from a subtle approach of support with a gentle nudge to make things improve. Others agree when weaknesses are pointed out but seem incapable to remedy them, such as this induction tutor who said: 'I am not sure that C is actually reflecting carefully or deeply enough to affect change in her practice. She is ready to admit her mistakes but tends to repeat them.' Occasionally, however, one comes across teachers who think they're fine (great, even) when they're not and are oblivious to hints and any subtleness. When teaching is really weak, you need a different approach: one that gives a very clear picture of the position, which is not sandwiched or hidden within positive points. What do you think of how Lesson Observation 7 (Table 4.13) has been written?

The NQT, who was the subject of this observation, taught in what one would consider a favoured context – teaching only GCSE and A level in a selective school. She received a great deal of high-quality support throughout her induction year. Nevertheless, the

Table 4.12 Lesson Observation 6: KS3 maths in a special school (eight pupils and five support staff)

Introduction   Your lesson plan had the right amount of detail, and the learning intentions were clear. I think that it would be worth organizing a seating plan that all pupils and staff are aware of, so that the likelihood of certain pupils bouncing off one another is minimized. You planned for the introduction to last for five minutes, and it actually took four minutes for X to give out all the bottles. While it is good for him to be engaged in such 'helpful' behaviours, the time taken to hand out resources resulted in many of the pupils losing a degree of attention. 'Ten Green Bottles' was sung enthusiastically by staff, but I think that having it on CD would have made it a stronger start to the lesson. I was impressed by the fact that three anticipated their turn to knock the bottle down well, and wonder whether you could have made this even more dramatic by knocking larger bottles off a table. I was pleased to hear you address the pupils when sending them off, and you clearly told them who they would be working with, and the context of their work. However, I would like to have seen you give them clearer guidance about precisely what you wanted them to learn. For example, rather than saying: 'You will be working with A in the shop', I think he (as well as other pupils) would have benefited from being told 'A, I want you to give B the right coin to buy food in the shop'.

Main Development   I was pleased to see you using the classroom effectively to split the pupils up, and the screens helped to keep distractions down. I was also pleased to see the computer being used effectively to support learning and to enable pupils to use ICT to learn independently. I think that your SSA deployment was good, and with five staff for eight pupils, this is always an area that is going to be looked at. All your SSAs appeared to be clear about what was expected from them, and the resources in boxes meant that work got underway quickly.

It was great to see D and E playing a game alongside one another, and they took turns extremely well for the first few minutes. However, they needed another activity to move them on after ten minutes, as they started to fight. C is clearly finding life a little tough at the moment, and I think he needs something very different to meet his current needs. I think you should be as creative as you can in organizing his curriculum to include the things you know he likes given that you can provide one-to-one support. At the end of the session, I was pleased to see all pupils involved in clearing away their things.

Conclusion   In this plenary, you let the video 'do the talking', and you needed to be more specific about precisely what they had achieved in the lesson. This would show pupils that you, and the SSAs, know where they are, and where you will be taking them in terms of their learning, in future lessons.

Summary   Overall, I thought pupil responses in this lesson were satisfactory, and that providing the pupils with a wider range of resources would have enabled them to consolidate their learning and demonstrate their understanding even more. I think that the timings within the lesson were also satisfactory although the introduction needed to be a bit snappier and more dynamic and the plenary needs to be tighter in terms of the verbal feedback you provided. The organization of the classroom and SSA deployment were good, and I think that behaviour management strategies were very good, and a real strength of the lesson. These included sitting D on the floor when he hit E, placing D between your legs when he became aggressive, and also moving C at the end after he had gone for A. All these strategies worked well, and meant that disruptions to the lesson were minimized. I was also extremely impressed by the contributions made by support staff and it is clear that there is a strong feeling of teamwork in the class. I am pleased to see how you have reflected on points made in previous observations, and am sure you will continue to reflect as you continue to get to grip with the many challenges in this class!

Table 4.13 Lesson Observation 7: Failing NQT near the end of induction – Music Year 10

Notes made during lesson

Lesson started with register (10.35am), two of the 12 in the class were late. Boy argued with you about the punishment for no homework but you were assertive and stuck to your guns – good message sent to the rest of the class. Objectives written on board and shared, though in a bit of a nervous throwaway manner. I think you should share the 'Big Picture' of the lesson. You give back homework and tests – comments such as 'Good work', 'Well done'. Why aren't you assessing against the learning objectives?

Very exciting to have a Kenyan drummer pop out of the cupboard! He demonstrated drum rhythms for different ceremonies. The students were rather embarrassed, especially when you danced in your African dress.

The packs you give out look impressive but much of the structure is unfamiliar, such as the self-assessment. Everyone's awarded themselves A grades but I'm not sure how they judged that, and in fact they worked for a very short time and guided by you rather than independently. What is the point?

11.10 am One girl slyly eating crisps. I can see no evidence of differentiation. The students work in groups composing a polyrhythm – they take a while to get started, not knowing who to work with. The dominant boys grab the three big drums again. Could you organize this more fairly, e.g. one big drum per group? Some record their work, others don't. Why not share the assessment criteria before they start composing? You need to be firmer with the fiddling with instruments during performances. Why does the audience have no role in evaluation?

Plenary: Good to recap understanding of main points. Homework written down though not explained. Nice show of humour but it got out of hand and you lost control – you pulled the class back but no need to be so harsh.

Summary

Thank you for letting me observe. I continue, however, to have concerns about the quality of your teaching, which I've listed below.

1. Homework – some of the activities such as 'find out more about the sitar, tambura, tabor' result in fairly low-level downloading from the Internet. How do you know what knowledge and understanding students gain as a result? Be clear what you're looking for – 'Write about six different types of drums' could result in varying degrees of work.

2. Make connections to aid student learning: give the big picture of how the lesson is going to go; make key teaching points, e.g. about the rhythms; clear objectives. It's disappointing to have to be raising such basic points at the end of the induction year.

3. Be clearer in your instructions – tell them exactly what you want, why and within what time limit, and what the assessment criteria are.

4. Differentiation – in this group S, for instance, has a high level of musical knowledge but no more appears to be expected of her than others. In fact, she plays a maraca.

5. Behaviour management is improved but you need to be more consistent.

Post-discussion comment

We had a very long discussion about the lesson and your teaching in general. As a result, it is my opinion that you are not demonstrating that you meet the standards for the satisfactory completion of the induction period. In addition to the concerns from the lesson listed above, our discussion has made me worried about your lack of understanding of NC levels – you think these GCSE students are working at NC level 4!; reflection and insight into the effectiveness of your teaching; and responsibility for your professional development and the fact that you have not acted upon advice and very specific action points.

recommendation at the end of both the first and second terms assessment forms was that progress indicated that she would not be able to meet the requirements for the satisfactory completion of the induction period. The lesson observed was near the end of the induction year when tough decisions had to be made about whether she passed or failed, with the dire consequences that the latter would have – being deregistered from the GTC and thus unable to work in a maintained or non-maintained special school.

The lesson was not good, and the written feedback needed to make the situation clear – hence the tougher tone, which is less positive than the other examples in this book. The notes made during the lesson indicate some sound features of her teaching but the overall message is made clear in the summary and clarified still further in the post-discussion comment: 'It is my opinion that you are not demonstrating that you meet the standards for the satisfactory completion of the induction period'. Note that the writer includes the all-important qualifier, 'It is my opinion'. The final recommendation has to come from the headteacher and the 'appropriate body' at the LEA makes the end decision.

Most teachers find it hard to be tough, especially with a colleague but what gives me the courage to tell unpalatable truths is to think of the pupils. They deserve the best and should not have to suffer the consequences of poor teaching.

Observation has enormous benefits. Done well, it should provide an invaluable context for teachers to reflect upon and discuss in detail the teaching and learning that happens in their class. It should be an opportunity to have strengths and successes recognized, problems accurately diagnosed and areas for development identified. The benefits for the observer are also considerable. One learns so much from seeing other people's practice, and one can not help but reflect upon one's own practice and pedagogy. With observation we have an opportunity to really raise the standard of debate about teaching and learning, and increase teacher effectiveness and pupil achievement through the setting of valuable and informed objectives.

In the next chapter I consider how to help and give feedback on other aspects of teachers' work through looking at planning and work samples, for instance.

5

Other Ways to Help

> ► Planning
> ► Problems with planning
> ► Deploying teaching assistants
> ► Individual education plans
> ► Work samples

 I have a good student who plans well, is organized and friendly but she never asks for help or advice. I ask if there is anything I can do, get her, talk about but she says no. She hasn't offered to show me her lesson plans and I don't know if I should ask or not. Her lessons are OK but they could be improved to make them very good or even excellent. I know when I was on teaching practice I welcomed the teachers' advice. Does she think I wouldn't know anything? Does she think asking for help/advice is a weakness? Other teachers in my school think she might be a bit arrogant but I would like to help!

On average, primary teachers spend a quarter and secondary teachers nearly a third of their time on planning, marking and report writing (Bubb and Earley, 2004) so helping teachers become more effective and efficient in these areas is fundamental. This chapter gives ideas for how you can monitor and help people do their job by looking at their planning, deployment of teaching assistants, individual education plans, pupils' work and reports.

Planning

 Another NQT in the school is writing an A4 lesson plan for each lesson, with vocab, differentiation, and so on, as well as weekly plans. Her file is huge! I am not doing as much. I just use my weekly plans for literacy and numeracy. What is expected?

Teachers need to plan what they will teach and how they will teach it, but spending excessive amounts of time on long, detailed plans does not necessarily lead to better teaching and learning. The DfES *Time for Standards* (2002) says that teachers' time should be used for aspects of planning that are going to be useful to them, and which have a direct impact upon the quality of teaching and learning. Each school has its own views on what constitutes satisfactory planning. This will vary from school to school because the children will have different needs and because the skills, experience and understanding of the teachers themselves will also differ. All teachers need to be clear about what planning is expected of them, have their planning looked at and be given feedback that celebrates, gives food for thought and identifies areas for improvement.

Activity 5.1   Monitoring of planning

Have a look at a deputy head's monitoring of a special school teacher's planning below.

- What messages does it convey?
- List the key areas he comments on (for example, learning objectives).
- Are they what you would focus on?
- How are strengths and improvements noted?
- How are any gaps or weaknesses addressed?

Thank you very much for your planning folder. I was particularly impressed by the following:

1. *I like the fact that, in the absence of detailed schemes of work, you are producing brief half termly plans that show you (and consequently, your SSAs) know where you are going with each topic;*

2. *Your use of the new lesson plan format, which places the learning intentions at the top, is very effective. It helps to clearly focus on what it is that you want each pupil to learn during the lesson. The content of the lesson is much briefer, and gives a very clear indication of how you are introducing, developing, and concluding the lessons;*

3. *Your art (portraits) lesson plans – very good learning intentions for all the pupils;*

4. *Your maths lesson plans are also very good. The content of the lessons that you have planned allows for lots of opportunities for pupils to consolidate and develop their mathematical understanding. I like the idea of using the puppet to make 'errors' for the pupils to correct;*

5. *The activities you have chosen for science, art and RE are all very appropriate and allow for a range of differentiated responses.*

I couldn't see any examples of lesson planning for English – it would be good to see these next time please.
   All very tidy and thoughtful – thank you!

Helping people who are new to planning

Long- and medium-term plans should be in place in school, so teachers should only have to worry about translating them into lessons. There are a range of published schemes and websites that have good ideas, including ones from the Primary and Key Stage 3 Strategies. A great way to help people understand how to plan a lesson is for them to watch one, with a lesson plan to follow, and then to discuss the process with the teacher. The DVD *Teaching and Learning for New Teachers in the Secondary School: Interactive Study Materials* (DfES, 2004b) has a video of a Key Stage 3 history lesson with a reasoned lesson structure plan, showing what strategies the teacher uses, the teaching skill required and the learning gains he hopes will result (see Table 5.1). He uses mini-plenaries throughout the lesson: each contributes to making overall links and connections and to consolidation and extension, leading to the next stage in the learning. It would be useful for a new teacher to use the same model as Table 5.1 to watch any lesson and describe its structure, the skills used and what the pupils learned.

Using a pre-produced plan (like the one in Box 5.1) is another useful starting point but an off-the-shelf plan can cause problems if a teacher has not thought it through, understood the topic fully and adapted it for the pupils. I suggest that teachers imagine the lesson unfolding in order to allocate timings and make adaptations to a ready-made plan either because they have had a better idea, have different resources or because they want to take some pupils' particular needs into account.

Looking at the plan in Box 5.1, the objective (A) of the lesson is key. Teachers need to start with the learning objective from the curriculum, and then translate it into what they want the pupils to know, do or understand. Obviously they need to consider what they already know – that's where assessment feeds into planning. If they phrase outcomes as they would tell them to the class, they won't go far wrong.

Then the teacher needs to think of how to get the pupils to meet the objective, what resources to use (B), what activities to do and how to teach. What are they going to teach to the whole class and how are they going to do it (C)? There are so many different ways to teach anything so teachers need to choose what they think is going to work best for their pupils bearing in mind how long they have got, what room they are in, what resources they have – and the teaching style they are most happy with. Some people like to script what they are going to say, others just write down key points. Both are fine as long as the pupils learn.

What are the pupils going to do (D)? The most successful teachers plan interesting ways for pupils to learn and use a range of visual, auditory and kinaesthetic stimuli.

How do teachers make sure that everyone makes progress? Differentiation is hard but remember that it can be done in a range of ways, such as:

1. Same task that everyone does, with varying degrees of success;

2. Same task but with different expectations for different pupils;

3. Same task but with different time allocations;

4. Same task with an extension activity for the more able;

5. Adult support to enable low attainers to succeed;

6. Different resources to help or make the task harder;

7. Different tasks, but same objective;

8. Different objectives entirely.

Table 5.1   The structure of a KS3 history lesson

Strategy	Teaching skill	Learning gains
Visual starter		
Pupils are asked to generate questions about the mystery object shown and to offer ideas about what it might be.	Setting a challenge. Creating a two-part task for those who go beyond generating questions. Creating a positive climate, accepting all ideas, linking ideas to learning focus.	Involves all pupils individually. Activates prior learning. Encourages speculation. Creates an investment in the learning. Motivates pupils to make links and connections.
Sharing learning objectives		
Key questions are used as a means of sharing objectives. Key words are displayed for reference throughout the lesson.	Clarifying the area of learning in language that pupils understand. Linking the objectives to key words. Using questioning to ensure shared understanding before moving on.	Actively engages pupils in pursuit of the answers. Provides a measure of success. Defines learning outcomes, i.e. pupils should be able to answer the questions at the end of the lesson. Focuses learning.
Simulation		
The trade triangle is simulated by asking pupils to move around the room to designated points as if they were products.	Creating an assessment opportunity: the teacher can see who has understood, but pupils are supported because they can confer with those who have not been given cards.	Challenges selected pupils to demonstrate their understanding. Creates new links and connections through physical recreation of an abstract concept (trade triangle).

Sequencing Pupils are asked to sequence a series of pictures related to the slave trade – with or without using captions as directed by the teacher.	Careful planning of the task: the teacher knows both the benefits and limitations of the task (it is 'basic'); he or she plans for differentiation and challenge. Intervention using questioning to extend thinking.	Begins to link one sequence of causation with another (the trade triangle with the capturing of slaves).
Focused video sequence Pupils are asked to look for new pieces of information and note them on blank caption cards.	Using the video to build on the sequencing task; taking pupils beyond the 'basic' to the more complex.	Develops a more complex model (the sequence of causation related to capturing and trading of slaves). Develops a personal relationship to the area of learning; increases interest and motivation.
Final plenary Pupils are asked to present an aspect of their learning to the whole class using the OHP. Learning is summarized and linked back to the key questions.	Creating an assessment opportunity biased consciously towards those who are orally confident. Sharing learning gains.	Consolidates learning. Pupils share understanding. Pupils gain confidence in expressing ideas. Pupils see what they have learned.

Source: DfES (2004b).

The plenary (E) is an excellent opportunity to reinforce key points and to see how the pupils have met the objective of the lesson. This assessment will feed into the plan for the next lesson – and so the cycle goes on.

Activity 5.2   Differentiation

Ask teachers to think of eight ways to differentiate one specific learning objective and discuss which will be the most effective.

Box 5.1   Lesson plan

Year 6 Term 1 Alice in Wonderland (based on a plan from www.hamilton-trust.org.uk)

(A) Objectives:
Be familiar with the work of established authors (in this case Lewis Carroll) and know what is special about their work (Text level 4).
  Understand how words and expressions change over time (Word level 7).

(B) Resources:
Copies of *Alice in Wonderland, All in a Golden Afternoon*;

Video of *Alice in Wonderland*;

Literacy books;

Dictionaries;

Sheets of sentences with old-fashioned words.

(C) Whole-class teaching
Share text level objective: be familiar with the work of Lewis Carroll and know what is special about his work;

Brainstorm all children about Lewis Carroll on flip chart, looking at special things about him as a writer. Watch the beginning of *Alice* on a video. Discuss and make notes on flipchart about what the start of the story tells us about Lewis Carroll.

Share word level objective: understand how words and expressions change over time.
  As I read Chapter 2, 'Pool of Tears', children to write down all the old-fashioned words. Discuss words, deduce their meanings from the context, and look up in dictionary. What modern words could replace them?

(D) Independent group activities
Easy: provide a set of sentences with old-fashioned words. Children need to look up meanings and replace with modern equivalents;

Medium: provide a set of sentences with old-fashioned words from other chapters from *Alice*. Children look up meanings and replace with modern words;

Hard (teacher directed). look at poem *All in a Golden Afternoon* (Preface) highlight old-fashioned words, and rewrite as a modern version, keeping rhythm/rhyme where possible.

(E) Plenary
Listen to the new versions of *All in a Golden Afternoon*. Ask class to identify which words and expressions were changed. What progress have they made against the objective?

Activity 5.3   Analysing plans

Have a look at the plans in Table 5.2 for Year 9 English and Table 5.3 for Year 1 Numeracy. They were written by two successful and effective NQTs in their third term on induction, for observed lessons.

- What do you think about the level of detail?

- Are the learning objectives clear?

- Will the activities enable them to be met?

- Do the activities gel together in a meaningful way?

- How is the plenary used?

- Are the timings realistic?

- Can you foresee any snags across the lesson as a whole?

- What overall feedback would you give, or what further questions would you like to ask?

Problems with planning

Problems with planning have a very detrimental effect on all other areas. Here are some different types of problem that teachers may have:

1. Used to using different formats;

2. Needing to do more detailed planning than other teachers;

3. Doing too little planning;

4. Doing too much planning and getting exhausted;

5. Insufficiently high expectations;

6. Insufficient differentiation;

7. Not covering enough of the curriculum at sufficient depth;

8. Overreliance on commercial schemes or other people's ideas;

Table 5.2 Lesson plan Year 9 English

Date and Time: 15 April 08:55–10:35	*Subject*: English	*Teacher*: Mr B L

Class/Group: 9A	*Theme*: Developing writing skills

S.O.W./Programme(s) of Study: Exam preparation	*NC Levels*: 4–6

Number of Pupils: 27	*Boys*: 15	*Girls*: 12

Context of Lesson
As preparation for the imminent SATs examination, students are focusing on their writing skills and reviewing their performance in the recent mocks.

Key Teaching Objectives for the Lesson	*Learning Outcomes*
• Identify a range of connectives to be used as alternatives to 'and', 'but' etc; • Apply connectives to sentences and to longer passages; • Identify opportunities to use connectives. • Develop writing by marking and highlighting strengths.	• A range of connectives should be apparent in tasks; • Understanding of how to use/plan to use connectives in writing will be developed; • Will be able to identify good examples of writing based on grading criteria from mock SATs paper.

Pupils' Tasks	*Opportunities for Enhancement of Basic Skills*
• See over.	Literacy skills should be enhanced – writing and vocabulary.

Differentiation

Pupils with SEN	*Pupils with EAL*	*Differentiation Strategies*
None	F, Se, So, J	Kinaesthetic, visual and auditory learning styles. Extension of gifted and talented by combining skills in tasks.

Assessment
Informal during tasks. Worksheet. Homework – formative.

Time	Teacher Activity and Teaching Points	Pupil activities and tasks
08:55	*Starter* – Students to work in pairs to replace simple, repetitive connectives – and/but – with more impressive terms. *Refer to the lack of variety with regards to connectives in mock paper.*	Identify the need for variety and imagination in their writing.

Table 5.2 *Continued*

Time	*Teacher Activity and Teaching Points*	*Pupil activities and tasks*
09:10	Students to compare their choices by looking at the completed sheets of other pairs. *Encourage students to revise the list and to commit a selection to memory that they will use in SATs exam.*	Kinaesthetic learning and focus on SATs as a target.
09:15	Clear task away prior to next task. *Students to work individually to complete a cloze exercise on connectives.*	Develop their writing by building on previous exercise, forcing them to suggest their own connectives. *High-ability students could also develop the nouns into noun phrases.*
09:25	Refer to lesson objectives and confirm that we have identified a variety of connectives. *Model planning of writing to allow opportunities for connectives.*	Students to identify the need to present opinions and contrast ideas, as opposed to listing points.
09:35	Identify different aspects/facilities of the school: lessons, canteen, assembly, sports, clubs, breaks, school concerts, teachers and so on.	Each side of the class to consider different perspectives of the list: Left – positive Right – negative.
09:45	Model the manner in which feedback is given: one side makes a statement about an aspect of the school and the other side uses a connective to introduce a different perspective.	
09:55	Distribute two brief sample responses to the longer writing task.	Students to mark using the criteria, underlining any positive points. *They should aim to give each piece a mark but task could be differentiated for any that struggle – identify why one is better.*
10:05		Discuss opinions in pairs prior to feedback to class.
10:10	Feedback on the passages and comments about the features that they have identified as those they could copy/use.	
10:15	Set H/W Criteria must be emphasized.	Students to copy in their planners – criteria must be included.
10:25	*Plenary* – Game: I went into a shop and I bought a . . .	Use of noun phrases – a crumbling, crooked carrot.

Table 5.2 *Continued*

Homework
Complete a revised version of the longer writing task.
Criteria:

- Any part that you think deserves a mark should be underlined;
- Connectives and noun phrases *must* be used.

Resources		*Key Vocabulary*
Teaching aids (TV and video)	Materials and equipment	Connectives
	Worksheets	Noun phrases

Teacher/Pupil Evaluation

Table 5.3 Lesson plan Year 1 Numeracy

Date/Time	Wednesday 13 April
Curriculum Area/Focus	Numeracy

To be shared with pupils orally and visually:
Amethysts, diamonds and emeralds: to recognize the number that is ten more or ten less than a given number 1–100.
Rubies: To recognize a number one less than a given number and one more than a given number.
Sapphires: to order numbers and write numbers 1–20.

Prior Learning
Children have spent the two lessons prior to this learning to count one less and one more, and recognizing the number ten less and more.

Key Questions
Which way do we need to count on the number grid?
Is . . . more or less than . . .? How many more or less?

Key Vocabulary
More, less, count on, count back, how many?

Resources
Large number grid on the white board, spider, tub, counters, number cards.

Activities
Mental warm-up:
To count on and back in ones from any two digit number.
Ask a child to choose a two-digit number. Children to close their eyes. Using an empty pot and

Table 5.3 *Continued*

counters. Tell the children that each time a counter is dropped into the pot they must count in ones from the chosen starter number. Repeat using different numbers.

Main activity:
Ask a child to choose a number from one to 50. On the interactive white board point to the number on the number grid. Remind children how to find one more, one less and ten more and ten less. Give pairs of children number grids and a spider. Hold up a number card and ask children to find that number on their grid. Children to find one more, one less and ten more and ten less. Repeat for various numbers.

Independent activities:
- Amethysts and diamonds: number cards one to 50 in pairs children pick a number card, record the number and then ten more and ten less than this number. Children will need their books organized into columns labelled number, ten more and ten less before the start of the lesson;
- Emeralds: Each child has a one to 50 number grid and some number cards one to 50. Children pick a card and match it to the same number on the grid. Colour in the numbers ten more and ten less. TA to check work before the end of the lesson.
- Rubies: Children place counters on five different places on a one to 20 number line. In turns children point to a counter. Another child to say what number is hidden, one child to say the number which is one less and one more than that number. TD
- Sapphires: order number cards 1–20. Place the correct number of counters on each number. Ext: Each child to make their own set of number cards by writing each number on a number card. TA.

Plenary:
Write the number 20 on the board. Hold number cards 1–50 up. Ask children to tell you if it's less than 20 or more than 20. Repeat using various numbers.

Homework Opportunities
Give children a number in their book and a list of numbers (vary the numbers depending on ability). Ask children to write the numbers which are less than the given number on one side of the page and the numbers which are more than the given number on the other side of the page. Ask children to practise counting forwards and backwards from any one digit number.

Assessment Opportunities
Can children use the number square to find numbers one less and one more than a given number?
Can children use the number square to find numbers ten less or ten more?
Can children find given numbers on the number square?
Do children understand the terms more or less?

Evaluation
- Aspects of the lesson that were effective and why
- Implications for future planning
- Do some pupils show a flair for ICT?
- Do some pupils not meet the learning objective and therefore need further support?

9. Using the activities suggested in team planning but not thinking about how to do them;

10. Not sticking to school plans;

11. Planning looks good on paper but the children do not make progress;

12. Weak parts of a generally satisfactory plan.

Subject knowledge

Some problems with planning stem from weak subject knowledge. To teach anything you really need to know what you are talking about and be prepared for those funny questions the children ask and all those misunderstandings you didn't think were possible! They will really test how deep knowledge is. If teachers are only ever one step ahead of the kids they will get into deep water – but it isn't easy. The number of changes, new strategies and developments mean that everyone constantly has to deal with new parts of the curriculum. New teachers have had a comparatively short amount of time to gain a great deal of knowledge, especially if they trained on the PGCE, which is a one-year course. Some will come with greater knowledge of the most up-to-date thinking on some subjects than experienced colleagues. Others will have gaps in their knowledge because their course was not able to give some subjects much attention. Leaton Gray's (2005) research found that the proportion of time secondary teachers spent on subject-based CPD, compared with the time spent on generic CPD varied considerably. Many teachers were not taking part in any subject-based CPD, some were attending courses relating to GCSE examinations only and in other cases, up to 80 per cent of teachers' CPD was subject-based.

Poor subject knowledge often shows itself in plans. For instance, in a 50-minute Year 8 history lesson the pupils had to go from finding out about totem poles to considering how the arrival of Europeans affected on Native American culture. This was too great a conceptual leap and showed poor planning that stemmed from weak subject knowledge. The pupils floundered. One boy had a brave attempt, saying: 'Totem poles became May poles'. Doh! But you can see where he's coming from: they're both poles that people dance around. How would you have responded? Let's hope you wouldn't say anything like what the teacher actually said, which was: 'Fantastic! Well done.' Can you believe it? So, not only does one pupil get a mad notion reinforced but 26 others think: 'Huh, I didn't know that' and the confusion spreads and lives on. Do you see how easy it is to do damage? Pedagogy is also very important. Teachers need to know how children of different ages learn best, and teach them accordingly. One of the hardest things I have done in my career was to take a reception class after teaching Year 6 for several years.

With all issues relating to subject knowledge it is essential to diagnose the problem accurately. Ask the teacher to evaluate their strengths and weaknesses, ideally with a more knowledgeable colleague: for how can you know what you don't know? People can improve their subject knowledge through reading and self-study – there are plenty of books and DVDs around to help. They can also talk to and plan with colleagues – great professional development.

Imprecise learning objectives

Many problems arise from poorly thought through learning objectives. For instance, a Year 3 lesson had the learning objective, 'To measure objects using centimetres'. I envisaged the pupils measuring pencils, rubbers, books and so on but they only measured lines drawn in their text books, which is a lot easier than measuring objects, especially as the lines were all in whole numbers of centimetres. It wasn't a bad lesson – most of the children learned something and got a bit better at measuring, but nor was it a good lesson. It was not very challenging and the children were bored. Crucially, no one met the learning intention because they did not have an opportunity to measure objects, so either the objective should have been changed or the activity.

Planning for mixed ages

Teaching ten subjects to 30 children for the year brings huge pressures, but those new teachers with more than one year group in the class face a particular sort of demand. Planning is hard because the national curriculum is organized by year group, not by what children are ready for. Katie Gibbs from Sudbourne Primary in Brixton has this to say about teaching Year 5 and 6 children together:

> There are three Year 5/6 classes so we plan together which spreads the load and is very stimulating. The biggest problem is that the range of attainment in my class is so wide: reading ages range from seven years to over 14 years so I really need to keep my wits about me for differentiated work. The more able Year 5 children benefit because they are able to 'chase the tail' of the older children. The experiences of the children in Year 5 are different to those in Year 6. For example, my Year 5s are weaker on coordinates than I expected so I've had to go back and then take them on. Luckily, the curriculum is really well organized because the school is grouped into Y1 and 2, Y3 and 4, and Y5 and 6 so we alternate topics on a two-year cycle. This works well but the Year 6 children need to have completed and revised all topics for SATs and I need to anticipate what the Year 6 children might be tested on. I often double up objectives by for instance writing letters that include an argument. My expectations of the older children will be different to the younger ones. Sometimes I'll start with the Year 5 numeracy plans but cut the number of days down and then fit in the Year 6 unit. (personal communication)

Deploying teaching assistants

There were twice as many teaching assistants in schools in January 2005 as there were in 1999 (DfES, 2005a). There are 147,400 of them compared to 431,700 teachers, which means that teachers have to manage the work of other adults as well as the learning of the pupils. Table 5.4 has some issues identified by teachers, with a few suggestions for solutions.

A frequent issue is deciding what the TA should do during the whole-class teaching parts of the lesson. This could be a time to prepare resources or for them to be involved

Table 5.4 *Problems with teaching assistants*

Issue	Ideas/solutions
Being unsure of the additional adult's role.	Find out exactly what they are paid to do; some are funded to work with individual SEN pupils.
Not sure when they are going to be in the class.	Find out exactly when they are coming and make sure they know that you're expecting them.
Not wanting to ask them to do menial tasks.	Again, look at their job description. Most are happy to help out.
Some do too much for the children and encourage over-dependence.	Model the sort of teaching you want. Don't be afraid to mention concerns – they haven't benefited from training like yours and so are usually more than pleased to be given advice.
Some have little control over the children.	Again, model how to manage behaviour. Speak to their line manager if this is a big problem.
Some can take over the class.	This is very tricky. Speak to them about the need to establish yourself as the teacher, but otherwise get advice on how to deal with this.
Some talk when the teacher has asked for everyone's attention.	Theatrically or humorously emphasize that you need everyone's attention.
Some don't do quite what you've asked them to.	Explain, model, write instructions; speak to them about your concern.
Some are stuck in their ways and do not like new ideas and practices.	Tricky. Try to get them on your side by asking for their advice, their patience in trying things out.
Planning for them, but they do not turn up.	Make sure they and others know how much you depend on and value them. Make a fuss if they are taken away too often.
They have poor literacy skills and spell things wrongly.	Deploy them to avoid them needing to write.
They don't use initiative.	Thank them and encourage them when they do use initiative, making them realize that it's ok.

with certain children – checking understanding, for instance. Even when the teacher is teaching the whole class, there is a role for the teaching assistant in oiling the discussion by drawing in reticent pupils, starting the ball rolling when they are slow to contribute and joining in. Teaching assistants can help to prevent and manage incipient behaviour problems by:

- sitting alongside a difficult child so they can be settled and involved;

- focusing the attention of inattentive pupils on the teacher by directing them to look, answer or apply themselves to questions as appropriate;

- eye contact, by sitting at the front rather than the back, so facial gestures can be seen;

- supporting children who need specific help to access the lesson.

Confident teaching assistants can help deliver the lesson. They might echo the teacher by repeating, rewarding or refining teaching points, for example by repeating or rephrasing instructions for pupils who are slow to respond ('That's right, look for the speech marks'). The most obvious use of teaching assistants is as an extra pair of eyes and ears for:

- observing individual pupils;

- noting who 'can' and who 'can't';

- picking up emergent issues;

- comparing notes and giving feedback to the teacher.

Most importantly, they need to know what the pupils should do and learn, and what they should do to help them. Additional adults have important information about the children they work with. They often know more about the children with special needs, for instance, than the class teacher. These insights can be tapped by asking the adult to make some notes about how the children got on.

Plans need to be explicit about the role of the TA and there needs to be some form of communication because it can be very hard for teachers to find time to talk to other adults who are working in the class. This often means that they are not used to best effect because the teacher needs to explain the activity and what they should do. A plan that can be given to them at an appropriate time should help (see Table 5.5). Alternatively, Box 5.2 contains a note that was handwritten by a teacher of Year 1 for her TA:

Box 5.2   Note to TA

Dear Mrs Humfryes

As we discussed yesterday, the children will be writing an account of their trip to the farm for someone at home. Would you work with the Circles (low attainers)? They have about six lines on the postcard. If you could, please:

- Write the Circles' addresses on the postcards while I introduce the lesson;

- Help keep them on task;

- Encourage them to use the sentence starters on the board, the picture cards on the tables and the sound/alphabet cards;

■ Encourage full stops, capital letters and finger spaces;

■ Use the white boards to spell any words or phrases the children need;

■ Remind them that it doesn't matter if they get it wrong as long as they try; that it is important that they can tell us what it says;

■ Feel free to help out other groups if the Circles are on track and working independently.

Thank you!
PS Hope the tea cured the headache.

Activity 5.4   Instructions for teaching assistants

■ What do you think of the tone of the letter in Box 5.2?
■ Are the instructions clear for what to do in the introduction, the main part and the plenary?
■ Are there any instructions that might be confusing or contradictory?
■ Does this give you any ideas for your own context?

Individual education plans

 My IEPs are written in 'teacher speak' – these are sent home for parental information. Pupils get them in 'pupil speak'. For some pupils, I write them in the form of short social stories. These are carried to and from lessons by the pupils themselves, and if they have achieved one of the targets on their sheet, it is noted, dated and signed by the teacher. This system works well. The pupils are involved with their targets, as are their parents, and progress can be seen by the pupils themselves as they have ownership of their sheets. They are very keen to attain their targets and try very hard.

I see such a range in the quality and use of individual education plans (IEPs) that I think it is important to help teachers with these too. IEPs should be used to take into account the pupils' needs, and will often have targets about things which influence their ability to learn, social skills, for example. When IEPs are neglected there are understandable consequences for the pupils. Giving teachers feedback on the quality of their IEPs and use of them might be a role for the Senco or anyone helping teachers develop.

Activity 5.5   Feedback on individual education plans

Read the feedback given by a deputy to a teacher of a secondary class of students in a special school.

– What do you think of the overall tone and level of feedback?

– What messages is it sending to the teacher?

– Is everything clear?

An excellent set of IEPs – well done!

I am really impressed by this set of IEPs, and it is clear that you have given a huge amount of thought into devising targets to meet the needs of all the pupils in the class. It is also evident that you have borne in mind all the information in the guidance notes, which (a) demonstrates your attention to detail, and (b) significantly reduces my number of amendments! I particularly liked the following:

- *A's maths sequencing target overarching different areas of the curriculum;*
- *The level of detail in B's English IEP;*
- *The 'step by step' approach outlined in C's PSHE IEP;*
- *D's English IEP – linking reading and communication targets together;*
- *Empowering E to use the whiteboard pen – very brave!*
- *F's playground target (PSHE) – very important;*
- *Empowering G to ask for 'more' (English);*
- *The introduction of a communication book for A;*
- *B's 'profile' of favourite interactive whiteboard activities (ICT);*
- *Extending C's use of PECS throughout the day;*
- *D being the 'register monitor!'*
- *E's comprehensive English target;*
- *Empowering F to ask others to 'stop';*
- *G's developing independence in the water;*
- *The thought and support you have given in the 'liaison with home' sections.*

Please have a look at B's Maths, A's English and D's PSHE targets for my comments, and amend where appropriate. Other than that, leave the rest exactly as they are!

Work samples

Pupils' work is a useful source of evidence about the effectiveness of a teacher. It is in many ways the proof of the pudding. It is easier to select the work of a few children of different levels of attainment rather than look at the whole class. Here are some suggestions:

Table 5.5 *Plan for an additional adult*

Name:
Lesson and time:

What to do while I am whole-class teaching:

Introduction

Plenary

Pupils to support:

Where and when

Activity:

What the pupils should do:

What I would like you to do:

What I want them to get out of it:

Things that they will need:

How did they get on?

Thank you!

Source: Bubb (2003b: 52).

- Ask teachers to give you exactly what you want and check that you have all there is – some people get children to use different books, folders, and so on in different ways;

- Have a focus (progress, standards, coverage, presentation, marking and so on) and a time limit;

- Look at a high, average and low attainer;

- Compare recent and old work to get a feel for progress;

- Look at plans to check learning objectives and the context of the work;

- Have level descriptions to hand so that you can judge attainment;

■ Compare three children's work on a certain date. This will show you how the teacher has catered for different needs;

■ Note down hunches and evidence then talk about them with the teacher.

Activity 5.6   Work scrutiny

What do you think of the two examples (Box 5.4 and Table 5.6) of written feedback to teachers, following a scrutiny of work?

Is it positive and celebratory?

Does it identify issues in a way that will encourage the teacher?

Does it identify what really matters?

Box 5.3   Pupil Work Scrutiny

Class: Y3/4 Sample Pupils: S and A

Your Language Skills books are a strength and demonstrate good attention to addressing basic skills. Marking is good with some very good features. There is clear evidence that both pupils have made progress since the beginning of the school year. There is a good range of work in maths: books are well presented and well marked. Home-Reading Record books were not seen. There is evidence of a good range of homework that is well marked. It was good to see that you are addressing basic spellings through the context of writing across the curriculum, but not making the emphasis so strong that content suffers or pupils are too inhibited to write. I like the idea of French workbooks for aspects of language teaching that are recorded, but check that the use of these is consistent across parallel classes. The range of recorded work in science in satisfactory and it is good that you have established a glossary at the back to enable pupils to record and learn technical vocabulary. More recorded evidence in science should be encouraged, without reducing the importance of practical and investigative work. Make sure that your timetable builds in enough time for this.

Targets for development:

■ Build in time for pupils to read and respond to marking more (start with selected pieces of work). Children need to be encouraged to go back and make specific structured improvements to selected pieces of work.

■ Try to ensure that you have more evidence of recorded work in RE and generally more opportunities for extended writing through topic/across the curriculum.

■ Expectations of recording and presentation of written work need to be raised. There is generally too much sloppy crossing out in books, space not used well and handwriting needs to be improved considerably. All pupils should be taught and encouraged to use joined up handwriting. These expectations need constant reinforcement in lessons and intervention – not just through marking (by which time it has happened). Similarly, the quality of work in sketch books is unsatisfactory. Look at how the Year 1/2 classes have used sketch books and used space well.

■ Make sure that you are clear about when to use Language Skills and Writing Journals. There is a lot of recorded work in Language Skills books and a limited amount in Writing Journals. Language Skills books are for spelling work, grammar and punctuation related activities. They should also be used for reading comprehension work. Writing Journals should be used for extended writing and any work related to genres, for example playscripts and so on.

Many thanks. Keep up the hard work!

Table 5.6 *Work sample using criteria*

Criteria	Comments
Does the teacher provide differentiated work for ability groups?	No evidence. All the children seem to do the same but there is evidence that the work is differentiated by the support given, either with a TA or teacher assistance.
Is the work of the average pupil age appropriate?	Yes.
Does the work match what has been planned?	Yes and there are cross-curricular links.
Are learning objectives clear?	Yes, they're written but some low attainers get little writing done because the LO are so long.
Is the work dated and in date order?	Yes.
Is the work marked according to the marking policy?	Yes, comments are positive but there's no evidence of children reading and acting upon them.
Is the book free from graffiti?	Yes.
Is the work neat and tidy?	Books are well kept, showing that children are rising to the teacher's high expectations.
Is there enough work in exercise books?	Yes, there's a range of topics and links to history work.
Strengths: High standards achieved due to high expectations – well done!	*Think about*: Abbreviating the written learning objectives; time for marking and whether children would benefit from different tasks.

Activity 5.7   What to do when problems are discovered through looking at work

Here is an induction tutor's note to the headteacher about her findings from looking at pupils' books in the NQT's class:

Presentation was poor, a lot of the work was left unfinished, the quality of work was poor and this was not noted in marking. There was no evidence of constructive feedback; very little evidence of foundation subjects being taught, and little to no evidence of AT1 in Science. There was evidence of differentiation but not enough to challenge the most able. Concerns were raised in the first term about the poor quantity and quality of work, and she seems to have made some effort with extended writing, but for this particular cohort of children she is clearly not challenging them, and expectations are low.

– What questions do you think they should ask the NQT?

– What issue should they tackle first?

Reports

 I'm just realizing that I am going to have to do a lot of careful observation of the class in order to write my reports. I have a basic idea of what each child can do but in things like ICT can they open a file? I assume they can – but have their friends just been helping them?!

Writing reports is probably the most important thing that teachers do because reports are read over and over again by many people, passed around families and friends, and kept for posterity. Even though we may think that much paperwork has little purpose, reports matter. What we write will last forever, and may come back to haunt us. The report on a nine-year-old who 'can identify and keep the beat in a piece of music' might seem embarrassingly like damning with faint praise when he is a famous musician featured on *This Is Your Life*.

Reports also form part of the induction standards that NQTs must show they have reached by the end of the first year in teaching. They must 'liaise effectively with pupils' parents or carers through informative oral and written reports on pupils' progress and achievements, discussing appropriate targets, and encouraging them to support their children's learning, behaviour and progress'.

Writing reports is time-consuming for all teachers, but for the newly qualified it can seem a mammoth task. Don't be deceived by computer programmes that promise to do it all – the process still takes ages. Speak to the teacher you are helping develop about how much detail to put in. I know of schools that go for something quite minimalist but others require a lengthy paragraph on each subject. The structure varies, too. Some have statements about the curriculum covered by the whole class, so comments are only made about each individual's overall progress. Table 5.7 contains a handy action plan for writing reports and here are some other suggestions to pass on:

Table 5.7 Report writing action plan

Name: *Date:*   *Date objective to be met:*

Objective: Write annual reports to parents that give a clear picture of children's progress and achievements.

Success criteria	Actions	When	Progress
You have an evidence base, i.e. you know what each child can do.	Collate assessment information so that you know what each child can do in the key aspects of every subject. Gather information from other teachers if necessary. Fill gaps in knowledge of what class can do. Give pupils a self-assessment so that you have insight into what they think they have learned and their greatest achievements.		
You know what the school expects.	Find out the school system for writing reports – speak to the assessment coordinator. Read some examples that have been identified as being good. Note stylistic features and key phrases.		
You have written one report to an acceptable standard.	Read the children's previous year's report. Write one child's report in draft. Give to the head teacher for comment.		
You have a timetable that will enable you to meet the deadline.	Set up the system for reports (for example computer format). Draw up a timetable of when you are going to write the reports, allowing about two hours for the first five, one hour for the next 20 three quarters for the last five, one-third over half term. Liaise with other teachers who are contributing to the reports.		
You meet the deadline.	Write the reports. Give them to the headteacher for checking and signing. Celebrate!		

Source: Bubb & Earley (2004: 90).

■ Build up a bank of useful phrases, particularly ones that express criticisms in a positive way. Read last year's reports to get a feel for style and talk to other teachers to see how you can be honest but positive. A phrase such as, 'She produces good work when she applies effort' sounds so much better than, 'She's bone idle'. Remember that even your most dreaded pupil is someone's baby.

- Think of the overall big message you want the pupil and parents to get before you get bogged down in detail. Having up-to-date records will help.

- Ask pupils to provide a self-assessment: what they are good at, have made progress in, have enjoyed, need to improve. Their views are usually accurate.

- Write succinctly. Try to make specific contextual comments to give a flavour of the individual. Reports should be clearly understood by parents or carers, so avoid educational jargon. This is easier said than done when it comes to talking about place value in maths, for instance. Start with positive comments before introducing negative ones. Make clear what the pupil has to do to improve.

- Draw up a timetable for writing your reports. Pace yourself – you can't knock them out in a rush. Choose a straightforward child to write about first to get into the swing, but show it to a senior member of staff for approval before doing the rest. One teacher wrote all his reports at once but had to rewrite them all because they were not good enough.

- Build rewards into your timetable – anything to make you stick to it. Believe me, the sense of achievement when they are all done is fantastic.
- Ask yourself
  (a) Have I commented on all the necessary areas?
  (b) Have I made any spelling or grammatical mistakes?
  (c) Will the parent/carer understand it?
  (d) Does it give a clear, accurate picture?
  (e) Is it positive?
  (f) Are weaknesses mentioned?

The next chapter considers how you can help teachers develop their careers.

6

Helping Teachers Develop Their Careers

> ▶ Opportunities within school
> ▶ Mainstream to special
> ▶ Applying for advanced skills teacher status
> ▶ Getting a new job
> ▶ Pay

Advice for teachers on career options is rare, yet it is so important as a way to develop. I'm guessing that most of the people reading this book help new teachers develop, and work with many trainees. In 2004–5 there were 38,270 of them, including 4530 on employment-based routes (DfES, 2005a) who may need guidance on applying for their all-important first job. But other teachers will also benefit from someone to talk through options further on in their career. This chapter doesn't attempt to cover all aspects of career development but focuses on options within school, moving into special education, applying to be an AST, the different steps to getting a new job and the complex area of teachers' pay.

Activity 6.1   What advice would you give to this teacher?

I have been a teacher for 10 years. Everything has happened quickly for me. For nine years, I have been a HoD. I have had a spell as an AST for two years and when that appointment (fixed term) ended, I was appointed G&T coordinator. I moved to a new school in January 2003, but this was a sideways move as I didn't know how to find my next challenge and regain my 'spark'. I have worked in three very different schools, but now I have NO IDEA what my next step should be, or what I really want. I have an interview on Friday for an assistant headship in another school, but I'm on the verge of pulling out. My heart's just not in it. I feel a bit lost right now. I never imagined that I would fall out of love with what I have loved for so long. But that's what it feels like.

Opportunities within school

There are many ways of helping teachers develop a career in the same school without just crawling up the promotion ladder, and which can give tasters of directions to go in, or enrich experience if teachers want to stay in the classroom. Developing pastoral experience might be one direction. Perhaps a teacher wants to organize a residential trip; work with pupils on an assembly, play, publication, school council, website or radio station; or get into counselling pupils or helping them with peer mentoring.

All of the activities below will be interesting in themselves and open doors to other career options such as advisory work, research, writing as well as leadership and management posts:

1. Leading school-based CPD or staff meetings and contributing to courses;

2. Taking part in a learning community – networking and sharing with a group of colleagues from another school or an online forum such as the TES staffroom;

3. Leading a subject or special initiative or rotating roles/jobs;

4. Carrying out action research in the classroom/school;

5. Writing for the TES or another publication;

6. Carrying out teaching and learning reviews;

7. Serving as a governor, union representative or on an interview panel or working parties;

8. Leading support staff;

9. Working on extra-curricular activities or projects with the community;

10. Taking part in case conferences on individual pupils;

11. Working with other professionals, such as education psychologists;

12. Working with an exam board or marking exam papers;

13. Mentoring another teacher such as a trainee or NQT.

Some schools are involved in 'Trading Places' projects where teachers swap jobs with someone in the same or another school for three days. That can be a great taster of another year group, phase or subject as well as a professional pick me up that many need.

Teaching a different year group or subject

One of the ways to develop a teacher's career without moving is to have different types of experience within the same school, teaching a different year group or teaching a new subject. Sophie Parker from Sudbourne Primary School in Brixton taught a mixed Year 1 and 2 class for the first time. You wouldn't think this would have been a big deal for someone who had taught Year 3 and 4 very successfully for three years, but she was aghast at how different it was. 'It was like starting all over again. My whole teacher persona had to change, I had to get used to a different curriculum and a completely different style of teaching'. The increase in daily contact with parents enriched the experience but added to the pressure.

She went from being very confident and knowing the curriculum so well that she could almost teach on autopilot to having absolutely no confidence at all. For the first half term she relied heavily on her colleagues – something she wasn't used to doing. In spite of the hard work, Sophie recommends changing age group:

> I have learned so much, it's massively rewarding. I understand children so much more and younger children are so responsive, so clever, so interested in absolutely everything – it's really very magical. I'm a better teacher all round now.

Mainstream to special

Sometimes people want to branch out into another educational setting, going for instance from mainstream into a special school. There are 13,580 qualified teachers in special schools, so compared to the 197,700 in primary and 211,100 in secondary you might think it would be hard to get into but at 1.8 per cent the vacancy rate is much higher in special schools than primary (0.5%) or secondary (0.9%) (DfES, 2005a).

With the inclusion agenda, isn't moving into special schools a recipe for redundancy? Certainly 83 maintained special schools have closed since 1997 reducing the total to 1088, though nine non-maintained ones have opened. Jon Sharpe, headteacher of Brent Knoll School in southeast London, believes:

> There will always be a role for special schools although the nature of some of their work may change: outreach work and support for mainstream schools will increase. Special schools have a key role to play in removing the barriers to achievement. (personal communication)

Nor is moving from mainstream to special a one-way street: teachers do go back into mainstream and are usually much richer for the experience.

Surely people need a special qualification? Well, yes and no. There hasn't been an initial training course for special education for many years. The last cohort of students doing the B.Ed (Hons) specializing in severe learning difficulties finished in 1990. Jon Sharpe speaks for most special school heads in saying,

> What we're looking for are highly skilled, enthusiastic and energetic teachers who relish the challenge of working with pupils with complex and demanding needs. Qualifications count for far less than transferable high quality teaching skills and the ability to develop effective relationships with pupils.

That said, teachers are now required to hold a relevant mandatory qualification to teach a class of pupils with hearing, visual or multi-sensory impairment but most schools will happily appoint someone without one so long as they are willing to follow an in-service training programme. Dr Hinchcliffe, head of Rectory Paddock School in Bromley, believes that school-driven professional development is ideal for teaching children with very special needs. In fact, there is so much learning on the job – so much peer observation and discussion because of the number of support staff and other professionals around – that many people don't realize how much they know and how skilled they are.

What sort of person do you need to be to work in a special school? Lynn Loader from Glyne Gap School in Bexhill on Sea, East Sussex believes that a good sense of humour and tolerance are essential qualities. But Jason Todd, an AST at St Giles School in South Croydon has a word of warning: 'Simply having experience of working with young people with special needs doesn't necessarily engender the right attitudes. A saintly do-gooding philosophy is not helpful' (personal communication). On the other hand, one teacher who applied for a job used words like 'retarded' and 'mongoloid'. She wasn't offered it!

Don't go to a special school for an easy life. You will be trying to teach pupils with the most challenging needs, the least predictable behaviour, who make the slowest progress. You always have to be on the ball – it's impossible to coast. Planning is hard. Even with small classes, history teacher Jason Todd has students on track to get A* at GCSE and others who can't read. He finds this challenge extraordinarily creative and loves thinking of dynamic ways to get hard to reach children to learn and relishes problems like 'how do I teach the Reformation to a child who is profoundly deaf and blind?' He also relishes having time to change behaviour rather than just trying to manage it.

 Being in special schools is fantastic; there is a real sense of community and a caring from the staff. Everyone is there because they love the job. The children are fantastic and each one is an individual and so very different. The steps the children make are small but magical.

Did you know that the chances of becoming an advanced skills teacher appear to be three times higher in special schools? Nearly 4 per cent of teachers in special schools are ASTs compared with only just over 1 per cent in mainstream. Why? Jason Todd thinks this is because 'in a special school if you want to fly you can'. Jon Sharpe thinks that special schools are developing their support for mainstream schools, which gives individuals plenty of evidence for the AST standards.

Applying for advanced skills teacher status

If people are really great teachers and want to stay in the classroom, becoming an Advanced Skills Teacher (AST) is a financially viable alternative to taking the promotion route into management. The main duty of ASTs is to be an excellent teacher in their own school for four days a week. For one day a week they have to share their good practice with other teachers and help other people's professional development – not only in their own schools but also in others.

If there is an excellent teacher on the staff they can apply to become an AST when they are still on the main pay scale. There is no minimum period of time that they have to have worked before they can apply to be an AST, and they don't have to have passed the threshold – I have assessed someone with only two years' teaching experience. However, the application form is gruelling and the applicant has to provide supporting evidence under each of the AST standards (see Box 6.1).

Box 6.1   The standards for advanced skills teacher status (DfEE, 2001)

1. Excellent results/outcomes

As a result of aspiring ASTs' teaching, pupils show consistent improvement in relation to prior and expected attainment; are highly motivated, enthusiastic and respond positively to challenge and high expectations; exhibit consistently high standards of discipline and behaviour; show a consistent record of parental involvement and satisfaction.

2. Excellent subject and/or specialist knowledge

Aspiring ASTs must keep up-to-date in their subjects and/or specialism(s); have a full understanding of connections and progressions in the subject and use this in their teaching to ensure pupils make good progress; quickly understand pupils' perceptions and misconceptions from their questions and responses; understand ICT in the teaching of their subject or specialism(s).

3. Excellent ability to plan

Aspiring ASTs must prepare lessons and sequences of lessons with clear objectives to ensure successful learning by all pupils; set consistently high expectations for pupils in their class and homework; plan their teaching to ensure it builds on the current and previous achievement of pupils.

4. Excellent ability to teach, manage pupils and maintain discipline

Aspiring ASTs must understand and use the most effective teaching methods to achieve the teaching objectives in hand; display flair and creativity in engaging, enthusing and challenging groups of pupils; use questioning and explanation skilfully to secure maximum progress; develop pupils' literacy, numeracy and ICT skills as appropriate within their phase and context; be able to provide positive and targeted support for pupils who have special educational needs, are very able, are from ethnic minorities, lack confidence, have behavioural difficulties or are disaffected; maintain respect and discipline and are consistent and fair.

5. Excellent ability to assess and evaluate

Aspiring ASTs must use assessment as part of their teaching to diagnose pupils' needs, set realistic and challenging targets for improvement and plan future teaching; improve their teaching through evaluating their own practice in relation to pupils' progress, school targets and inspection evidence.

---

6. Excellent ability to advise and support other teachers
Aspiring ASTs must provide clear feedback, good support and sound advice to others; be able to provide examples, coaching and training to help others become more effective in their teaching; can help others to evaluate the impact of their teaching on raising pupils' achievements; be able to analyse teaching and understand how improvements can be made; have highly developed interpersonal skills which allow them to be effective in schools and situations other than their own; provide a role model for pupils and other staff through their personal and professional conduct; know how to plan and prioritize their own time and activity effectively; be highly respected and able to motivate others.

In most cases, excellent teachers will have plenty of evidence for most of the standards but the last standard may be harder to find evidence for if they have not had the opportunity to help teachers develop. All candidates undergo a one-day assessment by an external assessor – people are not weeded out at the application stage though the assessor will analyse the form and draw up hypotheses to test out. The turnaround time between the application form being received and the assessment day is quick: assessors are asked to offer three dates within the forthcoming three-week period. Here is a real example:

22 October	Applicant completed form
3 November	Headteacher completed his part of the form
12 November	Westminster Education Associates offer the assessment
15 November	Assessor offers 22 November, 25 November or 1 December; agree on 1 December
1 December	Assessment day

The form should be word-processed and well written. You have to write sections on

- Career details – start with most recent and work back;

- Qualifications – start with most recent and work back;

- Professional development (CPD) – start with most recent and work back over the last three years, explaining how specific activities have improved your teaching and that of others;

- Why you want to be an AST;

- Examples of how you are demonstrating excellence in each of the six standards;

- Headteacher comments on how the applicant performs against each of the six standards.

Jot down examples of how you meet each of the standards. You will find that there are many examples that fit different parts so you need to decide which to use where. When structuring your writing think of how to be helpful to the reader, demonstrating each aspect of the standards, and don't include anything you cannot back up on the assessment day.

People have to demonstrate excellence against all six AST standards on the day so they need to make sure everything is ready and to hand. Beforehand, the assessor will agree a programme with the headteacher. The assessment takes at least six hours and is like an individualized inspection. It includes two lesson observations and interviews with the headteacher, colleagues, pupils, parents as well as the candidate. This is what an assessment day's timetable might look like:

AST Assessment Day Programme

8.00	Meet people; applicant show portfolio and explain data
8.20	Head Teacher Interview
8.40	Analysis of portfolio
9.30	Lesson Observation 1
10.30	Interviews with colleagues
11.00	Lesson Observation 2
12.00	Discussion with six pupils
12.30	Discussion with up to six parents
13.00	Interview with teacher
14.00	Period of reflection
14.45	Feedback

Applicants choose and can brief the people (pupils, parents, colleagues) whom the assessor will interview. They might feel tempted to choose the best behaved and highest attaining classes, but those are not always the groups that allow people to show off the most exciting teaching and learning. If things go wrong it is another opportunity to demonstrate more skills. When I was assessing in a special school, a disturbed 17-year-old was having his worst day in years. He threw a pair of scissors across the room, narrowly missing the heads of eight other students. The teacher caught them with one hand without interrupting the flow of her lesson, thus amply demonstrating her advanced teaching skills!

The purpose of a portfolio is to provide the best examples of evidence for each of the standards, in a form that is succinct and easily accessible to the assessor. The most successful are arranged in sections against each AST standard. Be selective: provide a sample and then a reference to other documents (for example, an excerpt from a scheme of work but then referring the assessor to a folder that contains more). A clear index, allowing easy access to each section is also useful. Obviously, not all aspects of the job lend themselves to written evidence, so make sure that the observations and interviews cover those. Many people offer graphs and tables that someone has said show that their pupils have achieved well, but which they don't understand and can't explain to an assessor! Consider pupil progress in terms of self-esteem and confidence as well as things that can easily be tested.

At the end of the day, assessors give their judgments in a face-to-face interview. In about nine out of ten cases, the outcome is positive. Anne French, a nursery teacher from Heathbrook primary school in Lambeth, remembers it being an emotional occasion: 'The assessor told me I was excellent in everything. It's the only time anyone's said that. It was wonderful, especially at that stage of my career – I was three years away from retirement. I cried!' (personal communication).

Getting a new job

I'm disillusioned teaching at a place with poor behaviour, a depressing environment, and a neglected music department that has no Year 10s this year, so no GCSE next year. I want to work in a school with flourishing choirs, orchestras, and a team of peripatetics teaching the whole range of orchestral instruments to a high standard.

People need to know what they want from a new job and why, and be clear about what aspects can be compromised if the dream job doesn't come up. Too often people are reactive, and search for the opposite of the context in which they have been unhappy, bored or ineffective without thinking about all the factors. Play devil's advocate. For instance, does the teacher above really want to move to a place where music already has a high status? Even if he found such a job, he would find it hard to make an impact since it is hard to change things when they are already successful. Perhaps if music is at such a pinnacle in the school, the only way to go will be down. Choirs, orchestras, instrumental exams all mean lots of management and hours of extra curricular time. Is he ready for that?

When on the hunt for a job, people need to get into the habit of scouring the *TES* and LEA bulletin job pages to look at trends as well as for specific jobs – often an addictive pastime that in my experience carries on even when one is happily settled in a job!

Adverts: reading between the lines

Experienced teachers read adverts with a degree of informed cynicism. Here are some not altogether flippant interpretations of real and recent extracts from job adverts in the *TES*. They might benefit the people you are helping:

'*Ongoing in-service education for initial year*' – this could be code for 'we won't let you out for any courses and you'll be completely neglected after your first year'.

'*We offer good promotional opportunities*' – few people can bear the school long enough to stay.

'*Highly disciplined school*' – lots of frog-marching, shouting and teachers who'd like to bring back the cane.

'*A new building is planned*' – the present one is a rat-infested ruin and it'll be years before that new building is agreed; and then you'll be trying to teach on a building site. Prepare for chaos.

'A rare opportunity to join the staff of this school' – you'll be the first new teacher in ten years, the youngest by 30 and be party to conversations about grandchildren.

'Be able to make a full contribution to school life' – you'll be expected to run lots of clubs and turn up at weekends to support the sports fixtures, discos and quiz nights.

'All classrooms are being fitted with interactive white boards' – note the verb 'are being' which means teaching over the sound of drilling; and you can bet they haven't got to your classroom yet.

'The role is suitable for an experienced teacher, an NQT or a GTP candidate' – we're desperate and will take on anybody who's quite good at sums.

'Excellent value added scores' – we're not great but the feeder primary is worse.

'Join this developing department' – the HoD is off with stress and several other members of the department have left.

'Improving/fast improving/rapidly improving' – measures of just how bad we were.

Application forms

 This is how I shortlist when we get hundreds of applications for a post:

1. Spend 10 minutes splitting them up into two piles: nicely presented/not nicely presented.

2. Now split them again into two. Personally, I would skim the qualifications section: throw out anyone with less than a 2.1, or a degree not related to the subject they want to teach, or Mickey Mouse degrees from Mickey Mouse universities.

3. You should have 30 or so applications now. Throw out anyone without strong IT skills and anyone without a grade A at Maths and English GCSE.

4. Now start skimming the supporting statement. Look for people with relevant experience, a passion for their subject, working with young people – people with get up and go, and who are literate. Throw out the rest.

5. Now read the rest properly. Split them into three piles: definitely interview; maybe; no. That should lead you to half a dozen candidates to call for interview.

Nobody likes filling in forms but people have got to do it well to get onto that short list. Here are some ideas to pass on:

◼ Make a couple of copies of the form so that you can draft it ensuring that you can fit things into the given space, neatly and with no mistakes. Check the closing date and work out when you are going to contact referees, write the personal statement, complete the form, check it and post it in time for them to receive it.

■ Skim through the form to see what is needed and whether you have all the information to hand. Remembering dates for all your qualifications and jobs can be a nightmare unless you have kept your CV up to date. Follow any instructions about sending photocopies, using paper clips rather than staples, writing in black and deadlines. Your employment history should normally start with the most recent unless the form specifies otherwise. Some forms ask for details of your recreational and any other special interests. Playing the piano is a big boon but don't exaggerate your talents – you may be expected to play in assembly!

■ How many referees does it ask for? Make sure you have asked the permission of whomever you choose and warned them of key dates, as the turnaround time is often tight. Not only will sending them a copy of the application jog their memories but it also means that they can reinforce and supplement, rather than repeat, information.

 Mention the school in relation to your own values, e.g. 'I was especially pleased to see on your website that Rentaghost Primary is dedicated to the education of the whole child, as this has always been my personal approach to teaching.'

Writing a personal or supporting statement is really hard. Start off by thinking about what the school you are applying to might want to know. Whoever reads your pearls of wisdom will be shortlisting against the selection criteria so consider using the same headings or order as in the person specification or job description, and aim to include at least one example of relevant experience for each thing it covers. Make sure you mention subject knowledge, professional development, planning, assessment, SEN, differentiation, varied teaching strategies, behaviour management, classroom organization, display, parents and equal opportunities. One way to do this is to write a paragraph for each point in the person specification including an example in each one. However, this can be boring and repetitious so try covering many selection criteria through writing about something in detail. Avoid unsubstantiated assertions and jargon. If you want to convey the sort of teacher you are, describe a specific lesson:

■ how you planned it following the curriculum but also using your knowledge of what the pupils could and couldn't do;

■ how you found out more, thought of how to meet the needs of a high attainer, one with special needs (using the individual education plan) and a child who speaks English as an additional language;

■ how you taught it using a teaching assistant and maybe some ICT – and why you taught it that way;

■ how you managed some fidgety/calling out/disruptive behaviour;

■ what the pupils (one or two instances) learned;

- how you gave them feedback;

- how you evaluated their learning and your teaching;

- what you planned for the next lesson as a result.

Remember that your supporting statement will be used to assess your written communication skills so give it a punchy start, a concluding sentence and make sure it reads well. Be relevant and concise – aim for one page, or two at most. Take care with the layout so that it looks attractive. Proofread it, get someone else to check it, and then check it again! The smallest spelling or grammatical errors might mean your form is relegated to the bin.

Look at the excerpt (the original is three-pages long) from Simon's application for a job teaching Citizenship, and my comments in italics. Do you agree?

> Dear Sir, [*Do you know it's a man? Better to address the headteacher by name in any case*]
>
> I would like to apply for the position of . . . I presently teach this subject discreetly [*discretely! Such a spelling error will normally send your application straight to the bin*] after pursuing [*undertaking*] a PGCE in Citizenship. I am excited about the potential for demonstrating my experience, energy and commitment in the development of Citizenship as a new and energizing subject in an environment that will offer a professional challenge and sense of personal reward. [*Yawn! Lots of jargon here*] I feel that the potential for Citizenship is enormous as it offers an opportunity for pupils to engage in a relevant and motivational curriculum, which I could [*remove 'could' – you do!*] make accessible and meaningful to a diversity [*ugh, try 'range'*] of pupils. I presently teach Citizenship at KS 3, 4 and 5 [*tell me more!*] The nature of Citizenship allows the incorporation of controversial issues and debates that consequently I have been able to capture the imagination and interest of the diverse audience in a classroom. [*This sentence doesn't make sense and mixing assertion with references to what you do in your school is confusing.*]

Contrast it with an extract from Lucy's supporting statement:

> As an integral part of the children's learning, I have arranged relevant educational visits and visitors to school thus ensuring that the children gain important firsthand experience. An example of this was when I organized a visit to the local Mosque on my final placement for both year group classes. The children on this visit were able to find the answers to their own questions, which they had discussed earlier. On returning to school, the children were able to demonstrate their understanding through independent writing, which proved to be a very successful exercise. I feel that this example of my teaching endorses your school policy of encouraging pupils to become independent and self-disciplined learners. This encourages moral and social

development, valuing all people; this is in keeping with the ethos of your school.

Lucy's use of a concrete example brings the whole thing to life and gives interviewers something to ask questions about, because of course she will be shortlisted. Or will she? In contrast to the quality of her word-processed supporting statement, the rest of the form looks appalling. She completed it by hand in the most atrocious, uneven handwriting with words crossed out and bits crammed into the bottom of boxes because she hadn't done a draft in pencil to see how she could fit everything in neatly. Her GCSEs and A levels are poor, although she has a decent degree and a PGCE, so she should have arranged her qualifications to draw attention away from the GCSEs and A levels. She even listed her two attempts to get English language GCSE rather than just including her B grade. There's such a thing as being too honest!

Teaching at interview

Lots of job interviews nowadays expect people to demonstrate their teaching with a class at the prospective school. This can be very artificial and some people seem to be offended by being asked, but without it schools would be appointing purely on the basis of interview technique. Anyone can have a shiny application and lots of people are good at interview, but teaching is, after all, what they will be getting paid for.

Consider what the interviewers are looking for. Basically, they want to see you can teach: snazzy activities and resources are a bonus but focus on the basics. I would try and tick all the boxes – read the person specification and try to give them what they want. Think about how you can show that you are professional, have a rapport with children and manage them well, are enthusiastic, plan well, use effective teaching strategies, and reflect on learning and teaching.

Plan a snappy starter that assesses current levels of understanding; have clear learning objectives; a main part that teaches them something new or helps them revise their learning; and then a plenary that enables you to assess their progress.

Schools vary in how much guidance they give on what to teach. Many give a completely free rein or something vague ('something for a literacy lesson'). Others are more specific such as 'Year 7 mixed ability French: recap hobbies and the present tense' or 'Year 9: a 50 min lesson on recipe development for a pasta dish'. That's enough to keep you awake at night!

 When I was interviewed for my first job, the head was impressed that I asked the students to say their names as they volunteered answers to questions. Remember you are not going to teach a lesson – you are going to teach children. Introduce yourself, tell them something about yourself, ask their names, and engage them. Give them name stickers and use their names, look at them when you are talking to them and listen and respond to their answers. Always have an extra extension task up your sleeve in case the students race through your lesson, having covered the material a few weeks earlier.

There are so many ways to teach anything and, though you want to look a bit interesting, it is probably not good to do anything too adventurous while being observed with a class you don't know. It is better to teach a standard lesson well than have chaos. Mind you, let your observers know of all the fabulous ideas you had. Keep the lesson simple and do it well. Give the interviewers a word-processed copy of your plan but check it for spelling errors beforehand. Make sure you have a plainly phrased learning objective, and some motivating activities that will allow the kids to meet it. Bring your own (or borrowed) resources rather than assuming that the classroom will have them – why are there never board markers that work? Find out the name of a child who is very able and one with special needs (any more than two and you will forget). Think of questions that will be appropriate for each. Make lots of eye contact with the pupils, smile, and use praise to reinforce the behaviour you want.

Afterwards, reflect on the lesson honestly and intelligently showing that you can assess pupils' answers, and think of ways to improve your teaching. No one expects you to be perfect, but your interviewers want to see that you are enthusiastic, and reflective. Lastly, be modest when it goes superbly – they are a lovely class, aren't they, and must have been so well trained!

> I had to do a 20-minute lesson on colour theory. I prepared a laminated colour wheel with Velcro pieces and had a quick interactive colour theory quiz. Then the kids had to get into groups of four and produce colour wheels by cutting up paint charts. I set it like a challenge: each team had to complete their colour chart in 10 minutes! For extension work I got some kids to consider tones and hues within the colour wheel. I had each team's equipment in trays so clearing up was just a case of chucking everything in the trays. It was a great lesson – the kids loved it, the observers loved it – but the job went to someone else!

Portfolios

> On my course we were told not to bother taking portfolios as they're not considered important but I'm sure that I got my job on the strength of mine – and no one else had one.

No interview outfit is complete nowadays without a smart little portfolio. Even if no one looks at it, carrying one will give you that all-important injection of confidence. Like feeling right in the clothes you wear to interview, it will give you the extra inch that means you get the job rather than being the oh so frustrating close second.

> So far I've put in my qualification certificates, CV and a mixture of lesson plans – mainly literacy and numeracy, but also science, history etc. to show my planning skills across the curriculum. I'm also going to put in a few photos.

Don't go for the kitchen sink approach. Look at things from the interviewer's perspective. They haven't got long to interview you – and they will not want to spend time leafing through a heavy folder. What do they want to know? You can make all the assertions under the sun about what a great teacher or leader you are but nothing speaks stronger than a concrete example. So, just choose one lesson or project that is illustrative of the best you can do – for variety, ideally not the same as one you wrote about in your application. The plan should be detailed to hit all the right notes (clear learning objective, assessment criteria, IEPs, deployment of assistants and so on); examples of resources; photos; a range of work that came out of it which is marked in an exemplary fashion; and an evaluation of the learning, your teaching and next steps.

We are talking about no more than ten pieces in all – go for quality not quantity, not loads of scrappy bits and bobs. Make sure it contains not only tip-top content but also presentation so that it sends messages about your personal high standards, and reflects your organization, literacy and ICT skills. One teacher scanned pieces of pupils' work on to glossy A4 photographic paper. The cover should be visually appealing, so that people will want to look inside: even if they don't have time to, they will assume something stunning lies within. Make sure that it is properly secured in a folder or ring binder. One teacher admitted: 'Mine slid out of the folder and all over the head's office'. Well, she made an impression but not the one intended!

Have the confidence to draw on sections of the portfolio when you are answering questions. So, you are asked about inclusion and hey presto, you can talk about how you met the needs of the autistic boy with hearing problems, showing the plan, the resources, and his work.

Interviews

 I seem to go blank and turn into a bit of a mute when faced with a headteacher!!!

Interviews vary in how formal they are and how long they last. Relax and do your best. Consider questions before answering and don't be frightened of a few seconds' silence – it is better than gabbling nervously. If you're stumped, smile and ask them to repeat the question. You're likely to be asked questions along similar lines to the ones below so you can think through answers beforehand.

- Why did you decide to become a teacher?
- Why do you want to work in this school?
- What makes a good classroom?
- Describe a lesson you have taught that went well.
- How you would handle some difficult behaviour?
- How you would handle difficult parents. 'If a parent came storming across the playground towards you what would you do?'

- Tell us about an aspect of your teaching practice you described in your statement.

- How would you ensure that all children were treated equally in your class?

- How would you like to work with parents?

- How do you approach planning and assessment?

- How do you plan to keep up-to-date in your specialist subject?

- How would you encourage children to learn?

- Give an example of how you have worked in a team.

- How would you go about building up relationships with other members of staff?

- What are you passionate about?

- Would you accept the job if it was offered to you?

You will also be asked if you have any questions. You do, and will have written them down if you want to come across as bright and proactive. Ask about the school's professional development.

Sometimes you will be asked a strange question that you can't see any purpose to, no matter how you try. One teacher remembers a strange governor who asked: 'Where do you live?' and then followed her response up with 'What's your favourite restaurant?' and a discussion of Thai food. Bizarre! Even odder was the headteacher whose second question of a male teacher was what football team he supported. When he answered 'Arsenal', she leaned out of the door and shouted to the schoolkeeper: 'Pete, we've got a Gooner here!' It was the start of a beautiful relationship with a staffroom full of Chelsea fans.

 I've just turned down a job offer at a school I really liked the look of: it had a superb reputation and had all the things I wanted in a school. However, walking around and meeting some of the other teachers, I just never got the 'Yes, this is the place for me' feeling.

You will usually be offered the job on the day or soon afterwards and people expect an immediate answer, but having a day to think about it is acceptable. Say you will accept, *subject to a satisfactory contract and salary*, so that you get a fair deal.

Pay

Teachers' pay is really confusing because there have been so many changes. The figures in this book relate to September 2005 but if you want to keep up-to-date go to http://www.teachernet.gov.uk/pay The site has a handy online pay calculator that will work out salaries. For a start, people need to understand that there are different pay scales for:

- Unqualified teachers;

- Main scale;

- Upper scale;

- Advanced skills teachers;

- Leadership group;

- Headteachers.

Within each of these there are four separate scales (London weighting is no more) depending on whether you work in inner, outer or the fringe of London or elsewhere in England and Wales. Of the 33 London boroughs, those that border a county get outer London pay and all others get inner London. So, most of Hertfordshire is classed as England and Wales but in parts of it such as Welwyn and Hatfield you will get fringe pay; Barnet, Enfield and Harrow are in outer London; and Camden and Brent are classed as inner London. There's nearly £4000 difference between the areas so it pays to be strategic. Ealing, Haringey and Merton are classed as inner London, even though they are not in the inner ring. It is hard to find easy rules about fringe payments so the best thing to do is to contact the LEA or local union braches.

Unqualified teachers

In 2004 there were 17,660 people working as teachers in our schools who didn't have qualified teacher status. This is a massive increase since 2000 when there were just 3810 (DfES, 2005a). They include instructors, people who trained overseas and those on employment-based routes to qualified teacher status such as the graduate teacher programme. These people are paid on the ten-point unqualified teacher scale, the top of which is actually higher than the start of the main pay scale for qualified teachers. In fact at £25,818 in inner London and £22,203 in England and Wales, it is just below what people on M3 get (see Table 6.1).

Main pay scale

All qualified teachers start on the Main Pay Scale – some adverts refer to its old names: CPS, common pay spine or TPS, teachers' pay scale. Teachers on the main pay scale move up a point every year (subject to satisfactory progress), in September. Part-time and temporary teachers also go up a point so long as they have been employed for at least 26 weeks during the year.

Most people start on M1 and after six years will be at the top of the scale M6 but it's essential for them to negotiate a fair starting point when they get their first job because teachers can start higher up the scale in recognition of 'relevant' experience. However, you have got to be proactive about asking. One 46-year-old mother of four with 20 years of rich experience as a nursery nurse and a first class BEd assumed that the school would automatically pay her more but they didn't. She started on M1, the same as a 22-year-old straight from college. Once awarded, experience points cannot be taken away even if people move schools.

Threshold and Upper Pay Scale

The Upper Pay Scale (UPS) is what people get when they have reached the top of the main pay scale and have successfully passed the Threshold assessment, which requires people to prove to the headteacher that they meet these standards:

1. Knowledge and Understanding: Teachers should demonstrate that they have a thorough and up-to-date knowledge of the teaching of their subject(s) and take account of wider curriculum developments, which are relevant to their work.

2. Teaching and Assessment: Teachers should demonstrate that they consistently and effectively:
   (a) plan lessons and sequences of lessons to meet pupils' individual learning needs;
   (b) use a range of appropriate strategies for teaching and classroom management;
   (c) use information about prior learning to set well-grounded expectations for pupils and monitor progress to give clear and constructive feedback.

3. Pupil Progress: Teachers should demonstrate that, as a result of their teaching, their pupils achieve well relative to the pupils' prior attainment, making progress as good or better than similar pupils nationally.

4. Wider Professional Effectiveness: Teachers should demonstrate that they:
   (a) take responsibility for their professional development and use the outcomes to improve their teaching and pupils' learning;
   (b) make an active contribution to the policies and aspirations of the school.

5. Professional Characteristics: Teachers should demonstrate that they are effective professionals who challenge and support all pupils to do their best.

Everyone who passes starts on point 1 of the upper pay scale and then movement through this pay scale is performance related. As with main pay, there are four separate scales depending on where you teach but the differentials widen by about £6000.

Excellent teacher scheme

Around 20 per cent of teachers currently on point 3 of the Upper Pay Scale are expected to be eligible for the new 'excellent teachers' payment, which comes into effect in 2006. As well as showing a 'substantial and sustained' contribution to the school, people will have to demonstrate excellent results and take on extra duties, such as helping with teachers' induction, mentoring and staff development.

Advanced skills teachers

Advanced skills teachers (ASTs) have their own 27-point pay scale, which ranges from £31,491 to £50,238 (£37,782 to £56,526 in inner London) at current rates (September 2005). Each AST is paid within a five-point range, which is based primarily on the nature of the work to be undertaken, the scale of the challenges to be tackled, the professional

Table 6.1(a) *The unqualified teacher pay scale from September 2005*

	Inner London	Outer London	Fringe	England and Wales
1	17,655	16,677	14,961	14,040
2	18,285	17,307	15,591	14,670
3	18,897	17,919	16,203	15,279
4	19,533	18,555	16,839	15,915
5	20,175	19,197	17,478	16,557
6	20,790	19,812	18,093	17,172
7	21,423	20,445	18,723	17,805
8	22,893	21,918	20,199	19,278
9	24,564	23,589	21,867	20,949
10	25,818	24,843	23,124	22,203

Source: DfES (2005b).

Table 6.1(b) *The Main Pay Scale from September 2005*

Spine Point	Inner London	Outer London	Fringe	England and Wales
M1	23,001	22,002	20,082	19,161
M2	24,315	23,316	21,597	20,676
M3	26,007	24,978	23,259	22,338
M4	27,756	26,697	24,981	24,057
M5	29,676	28,593	26,877	25,953
M6	31,749	30,642	28,923	28,005

Source: DfES (2005b).

Table 6.1(c) *The Upper Pay Scale from September 2005*

Spine Point	Inner London	Outer London	Fringe	England and Wales
U1	35,985	32,979	31,260	30,339
U2	37,752	34,101	32,385	31,464
U3	38,916	35,268	33,545	32,628

Source: DfES (2005b).

competencies required and any other recruitment considerations. ASTs can also be awarded extra points each September for high-quality performance.

Leadership group

Headteachers and other school leaders are paid on the 43-point leadership scale, which extends from £33,249 to £93,297 (£39,537 to £99,585 in inner London). Heads' pay is normally related to school group size, but governing bodies may pay more where necessary to recruit and retain headteachers of the most challenging and largest schools. Deputies and assistant heads are paid on a five-point range below that of the headteacher and above the pay of the highest paid classroom teacher. Members of the leadership group can be awarded one or two pay points in September each year, provided their performance is of high quality.

Teaching and learning responsibility payments

Management allowances have been replaced by a two-tier structure of teaching and learning responsibility payments: TLR1 and TLR2. For a TLR2 payment of between £2250 and £5500, teachers will have to show that they have a specific responsibility that focuses on teaching and learning and needs professional skills and judgment. This responsibility must be one that is not expected of all classroom teachers and it should be clearly defined in their job description. They must be able to demonstrate that their responsibilities ensure high-quality teaching and learning and influence the progress of many pupils, not just the ones they teach, normally through leading, managing and developing a subject or furthering pupils' progress across the curriculum. To get a TLR1, worth between £6500 and £11,000, you must meet all the criteria for TLR2 and be a line manager for a significant number of people.

Deductions

I know it sounds remarkable, but some trainee teachers don't realize that they will only get about two-thirds of their salary as take home pay. If they need an explanation here's one. Six per cent is deducted to fund the Teachers' Pension. The employer contributes 13.5 per cent to it, so it's much better than a personal pension and many people make Additional Voluntary Contributions (AVCs) of up to 9 per cent to boost it. All but the lowest paid work incurs 11 per cent National Insurance deductions. Tax is paid on any money earned over the personal allowance of £4895. The next £2020 is taxed at 10 per cent, and then the rest at 22 per cent. Any income over £31,400 gets taxed at 40 per cent. All qualified teachers liable to pay the GTC fee receive a single payment each year. Repayments on student loans kick in when people have earned over £10,000 in a tax year.

In conclusion, for the teachers being helped – for the millions of children who will learn more as a result – teacher development is crucial. Let us end this book with an ancient quotation that I find immensely powerful:

A leader is best
When people barely know he exists,
Not so good when they obey him and acclaim him,
Worst when they despise him.
But of a good leader, who talks little,
When his work is done, his aim fulfilled,
They will all say, 'We did this ourselves'.

Lao Tse

References

Barnard, N. (2005) 'We don't do predictable', *Times Educational Supplement*, 11 March.

Boyle, B., While, D. and Boyle, T. (2003) *A Longitudinal Study of Teacher Change: What Makes Professional Development Effective?* Manchester: Manchester Metropolitan University.

Brookes, G. (2004) 'I'm too old for party games', *Times Educational Supplement*, 9 April.

Bubb, S. (2003) *The Insider's Guide to Early Professional Development: Succeed in Your First Five Years*. London: *TES*/RoutledgeFalmer.

Bubb, S. and Earley, P. (2004) *Managing Teacher Workload: Work-Life Balance and Wellbeing*. London: Sage/Paul Chapman Publishing.

Bubb, S. and Hoare, P. (2001) *Performance Management*. London: David Fulton.

Bubb, S., Earley, P. and Totterdell, M. (2005) 'Accountability and responsibility: "Rogue" school leaders and the induction of new teachers in England'. *The Oxford Review of Education*, 31(2): 251–68.

Bubb, S., Heilbronn, R., Jones, C., Totterdell, M. and Bailey, M. (2002) *Improving Induction*. London: RoutledgeFalmer.

Coffield, F. (2005) 'Kinaesthetic nonsense', *Times Educational Supplement*, 14 January.

Collins, S. and Burn, A. (2005) *Teachers' TV Report: London Forum 2005*. London: Institute of Education.

Cordingley, P., Bell, M. and Temperley, J. (2005) 'Mentoring and coaching for learning'. *Professional Development Today*, 8(2): 15–19.

Cordingley P., Bell M., Rundell B. and Evans D. (2003) *The Impact of Collaborative CPD on Classroom Teaching and Learning*. London: EPPI-Centre, Institute of Education.

Dennison, B. and Kirk, R. (1990) *Do, Review, Learn, Apply: A Simple Guide to Experiential Learning*. Oxford: Blackwell.

Department for Education and Employment (DfEE) (2001) *Learning and Teaching: A Strategy for Professional Development*. London: DfEE.

Department for Education and Skills (DfES) (2001) *Advanced Skills Teachers: Promoting Excellence*. London: DfES.

Department for Education and Skills (DfES) (2002) *Time for Standards*. London: DfES.

Department for Education and Skills (DfES) (2003) *School Teachers' Pay and Conditions*. London: HMSO.

Department for Education and Skills (DfES) (2004a) *Five Year Strategy for Children and Learners*. London: HMSO.

Department for Education and Skills (DfES) (2004b) *DVD: Teaching and Learning for New Teachers in the Secondary School: Interactive Study Materials*. London: DfES.

Department for Education and Skills (DfES) (2004c) *Performance Threshold Standards Assessment*. London: DfES.

Department for Education and Skills (DfES) (2005a) *School Workforce in England*. London: HMSO.

Department for Education and Skills (DfES) (2005b) *School Teachers' Pay and Conditions*. London: DfES.

Department for Education and Skills (DfES) (2005c) *Leading and Coordinating CPD in Secondary Schools*. London: DfES.

Department for Education and Skills (DfES) (2005d) *London's Learning: Developing the Leadership of CPD in London Schools (CD)*. London: DfES.

Earley, P. and Bubb, S. (2004) *Leading and Managing Continuing Professional Development: Developing Teachers, Developing Schools*. London: Sage/Paul Chapman Publishing.

Earley, P. and Weindling, D. (2004) *Understanding School Leadership*. London: Sage/Paul Chapman Publishing.

Earley, P., Evans, J., Woodroffe, L., Coleman, M., Bubb, S., Weindling, D., Pocklington, K., Crawford, M., Neil, S. and Harris, A. (2005) *Evaluation of the Leadership Strategy of the London Challenge*. London: Institute of Education.

General Teaching Council (2003) *Teachers' Professional Learning Framework*. Birmingham: GTC.

General Teaching Council (2004) *Peer Observation*. Birmingham: GTC.

Guskey, T. (2002) 'Does it make a difference? Evaluating professional development'. *Educational Leadership*, March: 45–51.

Honey, P. and Mumford, A. (2000) *The Learning Styles Helper's Guide*. Maidenhead: Peter Honey Publications.

Hustler, D., McNamara, O., Jarvis, J., Londra, M., Campbell, A. and Howson, J. (2003) *Teachers' Perceptions of Continuing Professional Development*. Nottingham: DfES.

Leaton Gray, S. (2005) *An Enquiry into Continuing Professional Development for Teachers*. London: Esmee Fairbairn Foundation.

Malderez, A. and Bodoczky, C. (1999) *Mentor Courses – A Resource Book for Trainers*. Cambridge: Cambridge University Press.

Martin, J. and Holt, A. (2002) *Joined up Governance*. Ely: Adamson Books.

Montgomery, D. (2002) *Helping Teachers Develop Through Classroom Observation*. London: David Fulton.

Moor, H., Halsey, K., Jones, M., Martin, K., Stott, A., Brown, C. and Harland, J. (2005) *Professional Development for Teachers Early in Their Careers*. Research brief and report no. 613. Nottingham: DfES.

Murray, J. (2004) 'Never stop learning'. *Times Educational Supplement*, 16 January.

OfSTED (2002) *Performance Management of Teachers*. London: OfSTED.

OfSTED (2005) *Cameos – Examples of Best Practice in Teaching*. Available at: www.ofsted.gov.uk.

Portner, H. (2003) *Mentoring New Teachers*. Thousand Oaks, CA: Corwin Press.

Reeves, J. (2005) 'Securing systemic impact'. Paper presented at EMASA conference, Johannesburg, 11–13 March.

Revell, P. (2005a) 'Teachers get a sporting chance'. *Guardian*, 15 March.

Revell, P. (2005b) *The Professionals: Better Teachers, Better Schools.* Stoke on Trent: Trentham.

Richards, C. (2000) 'You don't have to be a genius but . . .', Letter, *Times Educational Supplement*, 7 January.

Riley, K. (2003) *Redefining Professionalism: Teachers with Attitude!* Available at: www.gtce.org.uk.

Slater, J., Shaw, M. and Paton, G. (2005) 'Unions' call to stop the scrutiny', *Times Educational Supplement*, 1 April.

Tabberer, R. (2005) 'We have to develop the best people business', *Times Educational Supplement*, 7 January.

Teacher Training Agency (TTA) (2000) *Supporting Assessment: Juliet.* London: TTA.

Teacher Training Agency (TTA) (2003a) *The Induction Support Programme for Newly Qualified Teachers.* London: TTA.

Teacher Training Agency (TTA) (2003b) *Career Entry and Development Profile.* London: TTA.

Teacher Training Agency (TTA) (2005) *The Teacher Training Agency's Role in the Future of Continuing Professional Development.* London: TTA.

Totterdell, M., Heilbronn, R., Bubb, S. and Jones, C. (2002) *Evaluation of the Effectiveness of the Statutory Arrangements for the Induction of Newly Qualified Teachers.* Research report no. 338. Nottingham: DfES.

Appendix
Photocopiables

Photocopiable 1: An action plan to meet an objective

Name:		Date:		Date objective to be met:
Objective:				

Success criteria	Actions	When	Progress

Photocopiable 2: Lesson Observation Sheet – prompts for looking at teaching

Observer:		Obs started . . . . ended . . . .
Teacher and Year group:		
Subject and learning objective:		
Prompts:	OK	Comments and evidence. What impact does teaching have on pupils?
Planning		
Groundrules		
Behaviour man		
Expectations		
Organization		
Resources		
Shares learning objectives		
Subject knowledge		
Explanations		
Tg strategies		
Voice		
Pace		
Use of time		
Questioning		
Motivating		
Differentiation		
Add. adults		
Feedback		
Activities		
Plenary		Time: . . . . Pupils on task: . . . . off task: . . . .
		Pupils on task: . . . . off task: . . . .

Photocopiable 3: Lesson observation summary

SUMMARY OF CLASSROOM OBSERVATION	
Teacher:	Subject, date and time:
Observer:	Focus of observation:

Strengths of the lesson:

Areas for further development:

Teacher's comments:

Objectives: To be met by:

Signatures:

Photocopiable 4: Record of lessons observed

Date	Time	Class	Subject	Observer and position

Photocopiable 5: Observation form – the QTS standards

Date:	Time:	Year:
Teacher:	Subject:	

1. PROFESSIONAL VALUES AND PRACTICE

1.1   1.2   1.3   1.4   1.5   1.6   1.7   1.8

2. KNOWLEDGE AND UNDERSTANDING

2.1   a   b   c   d   2.2   2.3   2.4   2.5   2.6   2.7

3.1 PLANNING, EXPECTATIONS AND TARGETS

3.1.1   3.1.2   3.1.3   3.1.4   3.1.5   3.1.6

3.2 MONITORING AND ASSESSMENT

3.2.1   3.2.2   3.2.3   3.2.4   3.2.5   3.2.6   3.2.7

3.3 TEACHING AND CLASS MANAGEMENT

3.3.1   3.3.2   a   b   c   d   3.3.3   3.3.4   3.3.5   3.3.6   3.3.7   3.3.8   3.3.9   3.3.10   3.3.11
3.3.12   3.3.13   3.3.14

Overall:

Photocopiable 6: Impact of professional development

Date and Venue	Professional development activity	What has the impact been?

Photocopiable 7: Observing other teachers – what have you learned? What could you implement in your classroom?

Teacher:	Year Group:	Date and time:

	What and when implemented
Arrangement of the room	
Resources	
Behaviour management	
Teaching strategies	

Index